G — Gentle
O — Observations
D — Directing
D — Decisions
O — Over
T — Time
S — Systematically

Every God Dot always came into my life at the correct and appointed time. God gently nudges us in the appropriate direction we should go. Then we have to make correct decisions to apply His guidance and nudges.

Occasionally, some of us need a smack instead of that gentle ever-present guidance.

Debra K. Linn

THE GOD DOT

SPIRITUAL MARKERS OF GOD'S DIVINE AND CONSTANT PRESENCE

LYNN BABER

THE GOD DOT

© 2021 Lynn Baber

ISBN 938836-34-3

All rights reserved. This book or parts thereof may not be reproduced in any form, stored in any retrieval system, or transmitted in any form by any means —electronic, mechanical, photocopy, recording, or otherwise—without prior written permission of the author or publisher, except as provided by United States of America copyright law.

Unless otherwise indicated, all scriptures are taken from the New King James Version®. Copyright © 1982 by Thomas Nelson. Used by permission. All rights reserved.

Individual God Dot quotations are used with permission.

With gratitude…

To the Lord Jesus Christ, my husband, horses, and members of The God Dot Facebook group who enrich my life and generously offered their support and individual thoughts of what God Dots mean to them.

To my editor, Vie, for her commitment and making this a better book.

For free resources visit www.TheGodDot.com

CONTENTS

Introduction	ix
1. The Arrival	1
2. The God Dot	7
3. Collecting Your Dots	17
4. The Dot Creator	27
5. The Dotted Line	45
6. Dot Drought	55
7. Types of God Dots	61
8. The Faith Gap	73
9. Enemies: Faith and Fear	83
10. Genuine Dots	89
11. Dot Blindness	99
12. Distraction Dementia	107
13. Why Dots Matter	119
14. Dot Erasers	125
15. Your Unique Dots	135
16. A Line of Dots	143
17. "Well Done."	155
18. The Path Forward	161
Notes	173
About the Author	175
Other Books by Lynn Baber	177
Afterword	179

INTRODUCTION

But blessed are your eyes for they see, and your ears for they hear.
Matthew 13:16

It isn't possible for two objects to occupy the same space at the same time, yet it happened on a stretch of two-lane road in central Texas. My husband and I were hauling a client's mare that was donated to Texas A&M University in College Station. Our rig was nearly fifty feet long, and the horse alone weighed over a half ton. It was midday with perfect visibility, steady traffic, and as many eighteen-wheelers on the road as other vehicles. Suddenly a white van in the oncoming lane jumped out from behind a semi to pass and filled our view through the windshield. With no time to speak or react, I figured we were about to find out what a sixty mile-per-hour, head-on collision felt like. This was going to be ugly.

INTRODUCTION

Then—nothing. We didn't feel as much as a breeze. The white van was now ahead of the semi and we were still on the road. No dust, no drama, no wreck. The van never passed us, never swerved, and neither did we. Both of us knew that something supernatural just occurred.

God Dots are markers in your life offering evidence that God's promises are true and that the power of Jesus Christ lives within you. Mostly unexpected, they prove that New Creations in Christ are never alone. The author of the book of Hebrews wrote, "For He Himself has said, 'I will never leave you nor forsake you'" (13:5). Jesus said, "Lo, I am with you always, even to the end of the age" (Matthew 28:20).

Most God Dots fall closer to the mundane extreme of the supernatural spectrum than the miraculous. Miracles are rare, but one God Dot I encounter regularly arrives in parking lots. When the day is cold and windy or my body is exhausted or temporarily broken, driving into a full parking lot at the grocery store feels like an uphill climb—until I see that the space nearest the door is empty.

God Dot. An unbidden grin crosses my face and I give thanks.

Imagine how bold and confident you'd be if Jesus stood beside you every day. What could hurt you, tempt you, or terrorize you with Him by your side? Immediately after Jesus predicted his coming betrayal, Peter boldly declared, "Even if I have to die with You, I will not deny You!" (Matthew 26:35). It's easy to be brave when Jesus is present, but hours later Peter's bravado

INTRODUCTION

died. He denied the Lord three times because he was afraid. The world without Jesus is dark and menacing, but that's not the world you live in.

Peter had nothing but memories and Jesus's words to comfort him. He felt alone because he was alone. Jesus faced condemnation and crucifixion, something Peter couldn't understand considering Jesus's power to perform miracles, raise the dead, speak for God Himself, and cast visions for the disciples going forward. This wasn't the end he anticipated, and throughout the horrible night following Jesus's arrest, Peter was alone, vulnerable, and his faith cratered.

> "We can all see God in exceptional things, but it requires a culture of spiritual discipline to see God in every detail. Never allow that the haphazard is anything less than God's appointed order and be ready to discover the Divine designs anywhere." — Oswald Chambers, *My Utmost for His Highest*

Believers place their trust for eternal life in the presence of Christ based on the promises written in God's Word, yet they have difficulty trusting Him with the mundane moments of life. Is God a faraway God or one more personal? That's the question a dear friend asked decades ago when she went off to college. Raised in a fundamental Christian church, she considered God more of a power, deity, and creator than a friend, companion, and someone who cared about the details of her life. She asked because she was planning her life as an independent woman and needed to know what role God would play.

INTRODUCTION

Do you believe that your faith walk with Jesus is established when you accept Him as Lord and Savior and remains much the same until the end of mortal life? Did God create the world and engage autopilot, or is He passionately involved in life's most intimate moments? Most believers think the answer lies somewhere in between. What about you?

One way the depth and vibrancy of the relationship you enjoy with Jesus is expressed is in terms of God Dots. They mark the places where God steps into your life and leaves a calling card. Some folks recognize them and say, "it's a God thing." These markers not only reveal how you got to where you are today but also provide guidance about the path God has for you going forward.

Trust in the Lord with all your heart,

And lean not on your own understanding;

In all your ways acknowledge Him,

And He shall direct your paths. —Proverbs 3:5-6

Have you met an angel or experienced something you can't explain in any other way except that God was present in the moment? Even if you have yet to experience a true miracle like sharing the same spot of pavement with another vehicle, perhaps there's a special song that comes to mind in deep moments of prayer, spiritual heaviness, or indecision. Sometimes a stubborn melody repeats in your head, you can't remember the words or even the name of the song, but suddenly your spirit lifts, confusion changes to clarity, and peace descends on you like a cozy down comforter.

INTRODUCTION

A while back, a friend of mine couldn't get a particular tune out of her head, hearing it nonstop during a week of challenge and insecurity. She couldn't place it and couldn't shake it. The next Sunday, the church bulletin listed a hymn she hadn't heard in many years that she recognized immediately as her song. As she sang, the words poured out of memory, and she realized they were an answer to prayer. When she shared this story with friends, the words of the song became God Dots to others praying for their own connection.

I love knowing that God is present and active in the smallest details as well as in the big moments that define and shape life. As David asks in the beginning of Psalm 27:

The Lord is my light and my salvation;

Whom shall I fear?

The Lord is the strength of my life;

Of whom shall I be afraid?

God Dots bless, inform, and guide you. They reveal where you've been, and when ordered together, they offer a glimpse of what God has for you going forward. Think of God Dots like signs on an Interstate highway. They tell you where you are, what's ahead, and the distance to your destination. They warn you of upcoming dangers, guide you through detours, signal wrong turns, mark rest stops, and let you know where services are available. Security on the road, especially in unfamiliar places, comes from signs you see and trust.

God Dots mark His presence in your life.

INTRODUCTION

You know you're in the presence of God when you recognize a God Dot. The more Dots you see, the closer you are to Him. Nicolas Herman (1614-1691), better known as Brother Lawrence, was a seventeenth century Carmelite friar who devoted every moment and ounce of energy to living in God's presence. At first, Brother Lawrence writes, it was difficult work because the temptation to distraction was so powerful, but he continued to practice until being consciously in God's presence became a glorious habit. Thousands, and maybe millions of people read Brother Lawrence's writings to learn how to practice the presence of God themselves. No matter his labor, his delight, or his pain, Brother Lawrence discovered the secret to remaining in the presence of God.

Any child of the King who spends even a moment in God's presence is humbled by His flooding power, love, and intimate knowledge of everything they are or were. The more you visit that place the more it becomes your greatest spiritual craving. In the presence of God, you learn where you've been, where you are now, and what possibilities await in the future. Most of all, you realize how deeply the Lord involves Himself in not only the big things of life but in small moments of importance to you. God Dots are everywhere and in everything because God is omnipresent. But, like Brother Lawrence at the beginning of his journey, few practice enough to see them regularly, much less constantly.

"That at the beginning he [Brother Lawrence] had often passed his time appointed for prayer, in rejecting wandering thoughts, and falling back into them. That he could never regulate his devotion by

INTRODUCTION

certain methods as some do. That nevertheless, at first he had meditated for some time, but afterwards that went off, in a manner that he could give no account of. That all bodily mortifications and other exercises are useless, but as they serve to arrive at the union with GOD by love; that he had well considered this, and found it the shortest way to go straight to Him by a continual exercise of love, and doing all things for His sake. That we ought to make a great difference between the acts of the understanding and those of the will; that the first were comparatively of little value, and the others all. That our only business was to love and delight ourselves in GOD." —*The Practice of the Presence of God*, "Second Conversation"

If the desire of your heart is nearness to God, intimacy with your Savior, and operating in the power of the Holy Spirit, it's time to look for God Dots. They serve as guides, the distance between each one revealing the state of relationship you enjoy with the Lord. The more God Dots you recognize, the clearer your vision of God's plan and purpose for you becomes. Dots allow you to evaluate where you are on the journey by the straightness of the line they form and how closely one Dot follows another.

Many Dots reveal themselves in hindsight. The first conscious marker of God in my life came when I was two years old and sang myself to sleep with *The Doxology*.

Praise God from whom all blessings flow,

INTRODUCTION

Praise Him all creatures here below,

Praise Him above ye heavenly host,

Praise Father, Son, and Holy Ghost.

—Thomas Ken, 17th century Anglican bishop and hymn writer

Knowing that the animals I adored praised God was enough for me to join in. When I brought home an *A* in kindergarten music my mother was shocked because I couldn't and can't carry a tune. Maybe my Doxology concerts were painful to hear, because she remarked on her surprise when I gave her the report card. I don't know if the memory is real or the result of my mother's comment, but the God Dot is still there.

My journey didn't proceed in a straight line and there were many early years during which I don't remember a single God Dot. Of the eight or more books I've published, this is the most personal, because I don't know how to share the power and possibility of God Dots without the stories. When you read about the many ways and instances that God left markers in my life, I hope they'll tease from memory stories of your own.

Some people might be content with the knowledge that God Dots exist even if they don't see them often, but I want more than that for you. I want to help you train your mind and spirit to see the evidence of God's love for you every day. Brother Lawrence learned to overcome the temptation to take his eyes off his beloved Lord, but it was a work of years even without phone calls, instant messaging, texts, and Tweets. It's far more difficult to maintain your focus now than in the seventeenth

INTRODUCTION

century. Today, distraction is the norm and unbroken concentration is remarkable.

After reading this book, you'll be better prepared to see God's personal markers in your life and to create a unique God Dot map you can add to every day. If you can't wait to begin your God Dot journey until you finish the book, jump on over to Facebook and join the private group, The God Dot.

God Dot: *A light on the pathway of life.* — Nan

ONE

THE ARRIVAL

Jesus said to them, "Do you believe that I am able to do this?" They said to Him, "Yes, Lord." Then He touched their eyes, saying, "According to your faith let it be to you." And their eyes were opened.
Matthew 9:28-30

Early morning sunshine touched my face like puppy breath as I walked under a limitless sky, woods to the east and suburban backyards to the west. It was a day like many others since we moved into town after more than thirty years in the country. These walks are precious time I share with the Lord before the day's schedule kicks in and my mind slips into performance mode. On September 5, 2020, the God Dot was born.

God Dots didn't begin that morning, but it was the first time that the precious moments when God makes Himself known in my life had a name, and I knew something yet unrevealed lay ahead.

Children arrive believing that they're the center of the universe and that somehow their perspective defines the boundaries of the world. Toddlers don't understand monetary policy, electronics, or betrayal. In their innocence, little children believe what they're told, step out in faith without pause, and love unconditionally because it's the only kind of love they know.

Jesus said that we must become as little children to enter the kingdom of heaven, meaning that we must accept without question, believe without doubt, and love without reserve. Toddlers don't ask for proof, demand identification, or comparison shop. Until they learn otherwise, little kids believe that Mommy and Daddy know the answer to every question and have limitless ability powered by inexhaustible love. In their parents' presence, children feel protected and secure, safe from monsters under the bed, boogey men in the woods, or storybook villains.

It's hard to reclaim childhood innocence and simplicity when you grow up in a world that worships the dark side of humanity instead of the joy God intended for us in the Garden. Because we can't walk with Him in the coolness of the day, we clothe ourselves in defense mechanisms and expect the worst more often than we anticipate the best. Once we experience worldly love that produces pain or breaks sacred promises, it's hard to believe in the limitless ability of God powered by His inexhaustible love.

Yet this is precisely where we yearn to return, to a place of connection, peace, and protection. We want to be wrapped in strength and to be in the presence of someone who makes us feel like our parents did when we were three years old. It's an easier concept to grasp for children raised by loving, faithful parents than those who weren't. Finding childlike faith for the first time as an adult is only possible by the supernatural power of God.

When I was a kid, the world was a safe place where children and their friends roamed the parks, woods, and town without concern. As dusk fell and shadows stretched to the point they disappeared in the darkness, whistles were heard up and down the block. Every dad had a specific whistle that his kids knew. When that special series of toots or notes shot through the evening air, each kid's brain latched onto it like a bee to its hive. Other whistles didn't concern them, but they knew the one coming from their father's lips and responded without thinking.

Life isn't that simple anymore for children or grownups. Families don't look the way they used to and too many children don't grow up blessed by protection, selfless love, and the security of a father's whistle calling them home at the end of the day. No matter the details of early home life, a difficult lesson for children of any age is accepting the fact that there's a bigger plan than the one they believe revolves around them. The world is incomprehensible to adults and children. No one can grasp the big picture, yet the worldly suggest that you're entitled to a vote in how your world is ordered or, at the very least, that someone in charge should listen to your suggestions and take them under consideration.

People are hard-wired to search for meaning, to make sense of their struggles, joys, successes, pain, and relationships that broke their hearts.

"Why am I here? What's the purpose of life?"

Bill Cosby asked questions for which there aren't great answers on his 1960's comedy album, *Why Is There Air?* Jerry Seinfeld said that this album motivated him to become a comedian. The questions are funny because we've all asked them and know how hard they are to answer.

Ten minutes into every road trip most kids begin whining, "Are we there yet? How much longer is it? Where are we going?" Creative (or desperate) families invent games to keep the children busy by challenging them to look for signs or markers along the way. We called it "I Spy." When a child spotted the sign and called out, "I Spy!" it was a small victory and proved that the car was on the right road. Every marker noted increased our faith that we were on track and moving closer to our destination.

When did you first wonder where you're supposed to be going and how much further away it is? God has a unique plan and vision for you but won't tell you what it is because relationship isn't about the destination as much as it's about the journey itself. You never *get there*—you *are there* every moment you stay on the right road. In some sense, God Dots are markers on your journey, boosting faith that you're on the right path and providing assurance that you're one step closer to your ultimate destination.

One hundred days after I first heard about God Dots on that morning walk, the manuscript for this book went to the editor. I wonder, what series of God Dots led you to read it? If you know, I'd love to hear your story.

God Dots: *I look at them as "justins" because they arrive just in time to help us deal with whatever's going on at the moment. God's time.* —
Casey Wilder

TWO

THE GOD DOT

But you are a chosen generation, a royal priesthood, a holy nation, His own special people, that you may proclaim the praises of Him who called you out of darkness into His marvelous light.
1 Peter 2:9

God Dots mark the places God makes Himself known in your life. You were created to dream dreams, see visions, and accomplish your unique part in God's eternal plan. No one else has your personality, talents, and potential to bring the power of the Holy Spirit and the kingdom of God into the world in precisely the way you do. If there were another you somewhere else, you wouldn't be here. God is the ultimate Creator, not only in power, but no design in His creative repertoire is ever duplicated. No two snowflakes are identical, and you are of far greater value than a snowflake.

God knew your life plan before you were born and designed a straight line from birth to death for both your benefit and His glory. Whether a lifeline or geometric line, each one is comprised of points or dots. If you could see every God Dot on your line, you'd cruise from the beginning to end as slick as my eight-year-old self whooping down a slide sitting on wax paper.

Effortless. Soundless. Joyful and direct, from top to bottom without a hiccup. Which, of course, never happens. From unintentional wanderings to rebellious rejection, no one walks their line perfectly. Conscious awareness of God arrives sometime after birth. Do you remember when you first became aware that He is there?

No one knows what they don't know. God places people and things around you that He intends for you to notice, but many of us don't know what we're looking for until we find it. Some folks are called to the sea, some to music, and others to medicine. Whether storytelling, invention, or planting corn, there's something inside you that seeks, but you may not know what it is until you bump into it. So much of modern life is reduced to routine that we stop expecting the unexpected and quit pursuing our call. God Dots help guide you toward the line God drew for you before you were a glint in your mama's eye. Where are you in your walk with Jesus Christ? Does God appear distant and aloof or is He closer to you than your shirt and shoes?

Every morning in warm weather, a friend of mine lets her horses out to the pasture, cleans stalls and rinses water buckets so they'll be fresh for evening. Then she waters down stalls and dirt to keep the dust at bay. Most mornings she sees a brilliant rainbow dancing in the spray bursting from the nozzle and thinks, *Cool. A rainbow.* One morning something different caught her heart, and she captured the rainbow bejeweled spray with her smartphone camera. What was commonplace before took on new meaning when spirit eyes saw the rainbow in the way God created it. That day's rainbow reminded her of God's promised hope and protection.

She recognized it as a God Dot.

> *The rainbow shall be in the cloud, and I will look on it to remember the everlasting covenant between God and every living creature of all flesh that is on the earth.* —Genesis 9:16

Why do some people see God in the mundane and coincidental things of life that others miss? For my friend, the difference may be chalked up to a change in expectation. As an active member of our private God Dot Facebook group, seeing evidence of God is becoming a daily event because she not only looks for His markers, but she expects to see them.

One of my recurring childhood dreams began around age six. The Ypsilanti, Michigan, subdivision we lived in boasted large backyards with plenty of grass to play Red Rover or Tag and a few delightful sand pits for creative digging. Few homes had fenced yards, so our playground was huge, comprised of three or four yards we considered exclusive kid territory. In the dream, I looked out my bedroom window toward the backyard. The house had a walkout basement, so my second-story window offered an expansive view. To my delight, the combined yards formed a beautiful green pasture inhabited by a herd of colorful ponies. Not black, gray, or spotted, but ponies of bright colors—red, green, yellow, blue, purple, and orange.

I don't know how many times I dreamed the same dream, even years after moving away. For those of you who aren't familiar, a passion for horses is often something you're born with that never goes away. That's me, although the opportunity to fully live my horse dream didn't happen at age six, but at thirty-four. The Crayola-colored ponies of my dreams were a promise of what would come later, an unrecognized God Dot on the line He drew for me.

Do you have a childhood memory suggesting a passion or ability you didn't recognize until later? What about recurring dreams? If you do, jot them down on a scrap of paper or tap a note into your iPhone. I'll explain why in just a bit, but please do it now before the details disappear into the fog of memory. Take enough time to tease everything you can out of your long-term storage files and include even the smallest remembered tidbit in your notes.

It's easier to see where God left His markers on your journey looking backward than forward. Using God Dots to look ahead is a formidable task unless you have enough Dots to form a relatively straight line. Maybe this whole concept of Dots seems far-fetched to you because they're tiny, and the significance of a Dot here and a Dot there isn't convincing. If that's the case, you've made a logical presumption—so let's dig deeper.

Do you have a smart phone, iPad, or computer? According to one source, the average person in 2019 had 630 pictures on their phone. The resolution or quality of the image you see on your screen is described using pixels, which is short for picture element. Combined in organized ways, these little bitty dots make up the images on computer displays and televisions. Screens are divided into a matrix of thousands or even millions of pixels. The quality of printed pictures is a function of how many pixels (dots) there are per square inch. Chances are, you haven't seen an unpixelated image in years. From great cinema screens to your car navigation display, what you see is nothing more complicated than a bunch of dots.

The more dots, the sharper the image. Anything that's high definition (HD) has lots of pixels. For example, a five-inch HD smart phone screen has more than 440 pixels per square inch (ppi), providing super clarity because all those little bitty dots add up to something amazing. A 2019 iPhone 11 cheat sheet (www.techrepublic.com[1]) reports that the screen has more than 2.7 million dots. Photographs are usually printed at 300 dpi (dots per square inch) which is the same thing as 300 ppi.

Whether screen images, photographs, or your Dot Line, clarity increases in direct proportion to the number of available dots. Old photographs reproduce poorly in print because they don't have enough clarity to pixelate well. Compare an ancient blurry photo of your grandmother as a baby with the one you snapped of your own granddaughter last week with your smartphone. The new photo is vivid and clear because it has many more dots than the old one.

Photographs and God Dots memorialize events for posterity by capturing the moment. Do you have a picture of you and your high school prom date? If you do, it's easy to relive the moment, feel the dress or tuxedo you wore, and if you're still connected, compare what your date looked like then with how he or she looks today. What did your father look like on your wedding day? What did you look like?

While unpacking the final boxes after a move, I found an 8x10 professional photo taken right after my husband and I were married in 1984. I had an idea of what we looked like, but over the years our older faces became far more familiar than the unwrinkled people in that picture. Yet, once I saw it, I remembered—what it was like to be twenty-nine, the necklace I wore and its special significance, and how handsome my husband was at forty-three. He's still a looker, but in a completely different way.

Memory is fallible, even more so as you get older. Curiously, more young folks have trouble keeping track of events, thoughts, and goals than in decades past. In Chapter 12, you'll discover what I term "distraction dementia," the phenomena explaining mental lapses in twenty-, thirty-, and forty-somethings. Memory challenges are no longer reserved for the elderly.

I remember seeing a small black and white snapshot capturing my widowed maternal grandmother and her second husband a moment after being pronounced man and wife by a prim lady pastor in the home parlor she used as a wedding venue. Another family photo from 1930 memorializes a formally attired groom and his bride wearing a gown that pulled out all the stops. If I had copies of those pictures, I could offer you better descriptions, but I don't. Memory is all I have to work with, offering hints at the interesting furniture and accessories I saw in the parlor, with maybe even a cat lying atop the upright piano, but that's just a guess.

THE GOD DOT

When you were ten years old, who was your favorite relative not living with you? A grandparent, uncle, cousin, or someone you considered family even if you weren't related by blood? What was it about them that earned a special place in your heart? Do you have a treasured memory of something you did together? Do you have a photograph capturing one of those moments? If you have one, how precious is that picture to you? If you don't, think of the joy of opening an unexpected envelope from a shirttail cousin containing a photo of you and that special someone, capturing the precise moment you still cherish today.

My favorite relative was a great-aunt's husband. They didn't have any kids and I always wanted to be the daughter he never had. Part of my heart belongs to Uncle Art because not only were we pals, but he believed in me when no one else did. He taught me how to hitch and drive a pony, saddle and ride a horse, plow a field by myself when I was ten, whittle wood and Ivory soap, gather eggs from child-hating chickens, and deep clean their coop. I wasn't thrilled with the chicken thing, but every summer moment on their farm was and is precious. I don't have one photo of him or of us together. All I have are fading memories and a church prayer book with his name engraved in gold letters on the cover. I'd happily trade the book for one blurry black and white photo.

Maybe you've heard of God Winks, points of experience of amazing coincidence. God Dots and God Winks are related but not quite the same thing. Winks are usually flashy moments that catch your attention while God Dots establish direction and build a story. I see the two differently because every God

Wink story or video I've read or seen tells an incredible story but doesn't link the Wink to a bigger picture.

To introduce the distinction between the two, I'll quote Steven Bradley, author of the book, *Design Fundamentals: Elements, Attributes, & Principles*, on the relationship between points, dots, and lines. In a 2010 blog post[2] he wrote:

> "The most basic form we can use is the abstract point or its concrete sibling the dot. A point is a coordinate without any dimension. By definition, a point can't be drawn. We can draw a dot. Dots anchor themselves in space and provide a reference point relative to other forms and space around it. A line is a series of points. Dots are about position; lines are about movement and direction."

LIKE GOD WINKS and God Dots, points and dots are related but aren't the same. Dots have function while points are simply there. God Winks are similar to points because they establish the position in time of a "coincidence" you know really isn't, but like any point, the God Winks I'm familiar with lack size and do not suggest direction. God Dots have dimension and serve as markers that you can use to construct a map of God's vision and purpose for you. Of course, maps are only as useful as the amount of detail they include. One or two God Dots may confirm your faith in Jesus Christ and the presence of the Holy Spirit, but they aren't sufficient to create a useful map. The more God Dots you identify and place in a line, the more you'll understand how you got to where you are today and where God may lead you next.

The map that best communicates God's vision and purpose for you contains many Dots, which means you must collect them. Memory is fleeting and unreliable, whether the subject is old family photographs or God Dots from the past. You lived the moment and saw the picture, but the power, value, and utility of the encounter naturally fades over time.

God Dots: *Signposts, not coincidences.* — Jane

THREE
COLLECTING YOUR DOTS

For I know the thoughts that I think toward you, says the Lord, thoughts of peace and not of evil, to give you a future and a hope. Then you will call upon Me and go and pray to Me, and I will listen to you. And you will seek Me and find Me, when you search for Me with all your heart.
Jeremiah 29:11-13

The purpose of *The God Dot* is to offer awareness and encourage you to begin your own God Dot map. There will never be a better time than now because memory is seldom perfect or accurate. Documenting each God Dot is equivalent to taking a mental photograph or video and putting it in an album you can open anytime.

God Dots are like the pencil marks on a kitchen doorframe marking how tall children are on specific dates. The more kids in the family, the more lines, dates, and names etched into the wood. From what I've seen, the people most interested in the record of how tall the kids were at various ages are the kids themselves.

"Was I ever that short?"

"Wow, I grew four inches in the last year!"

"I'm finally taller than Mom!"

The pencil scratchings on the doorframe create a record of progress as well as provide objective confirmation of memory. Who was taller in 2013, Daniel or Sarah? There's no argument or differences in memory because the doorframe tells the story. Do you remember precisely how tall you were at five? At eleven? One thing's certain, you can't go back and fill in missing information, like how tall you were on April 19th ten years ago unless you stood with your back against the frame while someone etched the record of your height on April 19th.

Height changes throughout our lives. For example, kids get taller and older folks usually get shorter. My grandmother was five feet, ten inches tall at age fifty but was closer to five feet, six inches when she passed away twenty-some years later. My husband was six feet tall for most of our marriage but falls a bit short of that now. I haven't checked my own, so I'm still five feet, seven inches tall.

Your God Dot map may begin with only a few markers, but the more you look for them the more you'll see. Awareness is largely a product of expectation. Like the kitchen doorframe, your map accurately records genuine history. God Dots don't have the limitations of time in the same way doorframes do, but they are still subject to the vagaries of memory.

Memory isn't reliable. Does God show Himself to you frequently or rarely? On days you feel alone, it's normal to believe that the Father is aloof, more of a faraway God than a personal God. But is that objectively true? Your God Dot map/journal is the best way to answer the question. The more God Dots you recognize the more you're likely to remember. Think of a time when you narrowly avoided an accident, injury, or storm. At the time you felt lucky but knowing that coincidence isn't an entry in the Christian dictionary, it's likely that what you experienced was a God Dot. Most of my God Dots became visible years after the fact. Filling in your map is a process of discovery and not the simple passage of time. Write down each one you remember now, including every detail of the place, circumstance, related events, emotions, remembered sensations, and diligently record every new one.

A few weeks ago, we enjoyed a couple of days of rain, a God Dot after a long dry season. Showers and light rain on Tuesday prepared the ground to receive what was to come. During noon Bible study on Wednesday the rain poured down in sheets. I'd just opened the garage door after returning home when a friend from the study sent this text, "Your creek is a raging torrent."

The creek is visible in several places along the trail I walk every morning. Earlier in the day I noticed that it had more water in it from the light rain the day before but not enough to get excited about. The deer living near the trail could still drink and pitty-pat across the shallow, easy moving creek without a second thought. I've seen the creek hours after big rains, but it was never anything remarkable. If it was a raging torrent now, I wanted to see it.

I drove around to the next street that ends directly across from the trail and the creek. My friend was right! I shot a short video out of my car window to share with my husband and friends. The cascade of water raced along like a bobsled at full speed, gushing, roiling, rising all the way to the top of huge rocks placed to protect the banks from erosion. It was an amazing sight, and deer would doubtless wait to cross until the water level and speed diminished. The power and volume of the water was beyond anything I expected.

When I visited the creek the next morning, only a small toy boat could navigate its unimpressive flow. If I hadn't acted immediately, I'd have missed something amazing because it was so short lived. The moment passed. Ours is a little bitty creek that barely moves, but I now have hard evidence of fleeting transformation.

Think back to a moment when you experienced God's brilliant light, standing high above the clouds on a mountain top of vision and connection. God Dots are moments that pass quickly before you return to your normal and familiar routine. Unless you record your God Dot, like my creek video, you'll lose the connection and may even doubt that it really happened as you remember.

When I left home on my morning walk July 13, 2020, I'd received both an important message and an introduction to what may come next. I've walked my dotted line for years but didn't always document the details of the moments when God revealed Himself and His plan for me. There are a few times when I believe God didn't intend for me to remember the message, and other instances when I was sure of the message but didn't write down the details in the moment. When I got home from my walk, I poured every detail, emotion, message, and element of a project yet to come into a WORD document because I knew I would need the record later.

That evening I told my husband, wondering if he'd think I was nuts. In what I recognized later as another God Dot, he was totally on board and more excited about the idea than anything we'd done in ministry over the years. We went to bed as usual and awoke the next morning to a normal day, which was when doubt shoved its foot in the door. Did I really hear what I thought I had? Who was I kidding? I'd never done anything like what I saw the day before. Maybe I'd blown it all out of proportion and God didn't really ask me to do what I thought He did.

In Chapter 6, "Dot Drought," I'll share the horrible way I handled a specific message God asked me to share in the book I (eventually) wrote titled, *Rapture and Revelation*. The instruction couldn't have been more precise, and I still remember every word He gave me. But as days and weeks passed the power faded, because after all, who was I to write this book?

I didn't repeat that mistake this time because I wrote everything down. On July 14, the day after I wrote them, I reviewed three pages of detailed notes and was transported back to the magic and power of the moment. It was real. My spirit exploded in confirmation and my confidence magnified a hundred times over when I read my notes. Even if the time isn't now, write down what you receive and treasure it. Abraham waited thirteen years for Isaac. I don't know if our walk and talk with God is more difficult today than it was then, but I know that making a record of what you experience matters.

When God makes Himself known in your life, write it down. Everything. Documentation in the moment is critical if you want to create a high-resolution map of God's plan for you. This is the time in which God has placed you and there is a reason. Don't trust something as important as walking out the unique plan and purpose you were created to perform to memory that fades over time. Prevent the natural erosion of confidence engineered by the ruler of this world, Satan, the deceiver, by making notes. You have an eternally assigned role that the devil wants to distract you from, and he'll use every trick necessary to get you to doubt your value, wander off your dotted line, and undermine your confidence in God as a personal, up-close Father who is with you now and forever.

If I didn't record the download from God on July 13, including the confidence and certainty I felt and the emotion of the connection and the clarity of the vision, doubt could grow unchecked. By documenting everything that went through my mind and heart, I could show up the next day and give a firm, confident answer to the irritating, predictable question of whether I really heard correctly.

THE GOD DOT

If I hadn't, I might have offered only a token bit of resistance to appease my conscience. Any voice that says, "Don't worry about stepping out, because if God really told you to do this, then He'll make sure you follow through," is from the liar-in-chief.

When you've had an encounter with God, believe it, cherish it, and act on it. When any of these doubts creep in, review your notes and kick them to the curb.

Maybe I thought too much of myself.

Maybe it was what I ate the night before.

Surely, God didn't just tell me what I was going to do and when.

Without documenting what I heard and felt on September 5 about the God Dot, you wouldn't be reading this, and I wouldn't feel as awesomely blessed as I do. What markers has God set in your life? Is there something you thought you heard, knew, or believed until normal life watered seeds of doubt that kept you from taking the next step forward? God's plan for you is real and that's a fact you can take to the bank. Create and maintain a God Dot map or journal. Invest time looking back to see where God moved in your life, whether you recognized it at the time or not. God expects you to chronicle what you learn and experience. It's the way to preview His vision for you and serves as an example for family and friends. If you have children, challenge them to begin keeping a journal of their own walk with Christ.

The Bible chronicles the appearance of God Dots in the lives of otherwise unexceptional people. From Jesus appearing on the lakeshore to invite Peter and Andrew to become fishers of men to the sun stopping its daily travel across the sky in Joshua

10:12-15, God wants to share every moment of life with you from the least to the most profound. Don't miss anything. Write it down.

> *Only take heed to yourself, and diligently keep yourself, lest you forget the things your eyes have seen, and lest they depart from your heart all the days of your life. And teach them to your children and your grandchildren.* —Deuteronomy 4:9

Respect and relish every communication and confirming event. They answer questions and establish direction. Sometimes, the line of God Dots you tracked for years miraculously transforms from pencil to ink. In my case, I don't discount the probability that there will be later tweaks, but it will take a big eraser to change what my God Dot map shows me today.

Compared to other God Dots I've noted over the years, those from the past year aren't exponentially bigger but provide the missing Dots I've looked for over the past five years. Once plugged into my map, huge gaps between other Dots miraculously filled in.

I'm more convinced than ever that documenting the moments and methods God uses to show Himself in your life is a critical element of understanding His plan and performing assigned tasks. If you fail to record your God Dots, the confidence and vivid clarity of the moment begins to fade the instant you do something normal or routine.

No matter what the nagging voice says, you're not kidding yourself.

Believe that God has a unique vision and purpose for you.

Do not doubt.

When I read my notes the day after writing them, I knew it was real.

It is real.

FRIDAY IS Share Day in *The God Dot* Facebook group where members are invited to post at least one Dot from the previous week. One member is so turned on to God Dots that she left this reply one Friday, "I haven't even posted most of my God Dots ... I'm not sure what's going on in my world, but man oh man it's cool!!!"

The more you see the more you will see. The more you expect God to appear in your life, the more you'll notice these supernatural markers and the powerful connection God Dots bring.

Earlier in 2020, I felt burdened with the weight of transitioning from youth, space, endless options, and from a beloved, comfortable, and familiar place to new territory with both the Lord and the world. I was tired and, for the first time in decades, had no idea what the next few months and years would bring. Events related to our unexpected move from our beloved barn into town caused me to doubt that I'd heard the Lord correctly on what would happen next. His Word is always perfect, but sometimes my hearing isn't.

I'd also prayed for rain to ease both a physical drought and the one in my spirit. The previous week brought a few showers here and there, but none to the *here* where we were. The forecast for the day was sunny and clear without the slightest chance of rain. Not long after leaving on my morning walk a small cloud formed above me and I felt one raindrop on my arm. One drop, unexpected and otherwise unremarkable except that it was a specific marker God delivered to release me from spiritual drought. Sometimes when you pray, "Lord, I beseech you for rain," what you need most is spiritual rain.

To me, God Dots are little windows letting His light through on my path. To brighten my day, to keep me from stumbling, and to clarify truth. — Laura

FOUR
THE DOT CREATOR

Then He gives us a tremendous, riveting pain to fasten our attention on something that we never even dreamed could be His call for us. And for one radiant, flashing moment we see His purpose, and we say, "Here am I! Send me" (Isaiah 6:8).
—Oswald Chambers, *My Utmost for His Highest*, Sept. 30

Dots reflect the Dot Creator whose powerful, personal vision and purpose prompted Him to create you—to bring you onto the stage. There are no duplicates, do-overs, or reused identities. God is the Master Innovator and the King of Unique. The dreams and ideas within you are there by design, to bring God's kingdom to earth. The ways in which He makes Himself known are unique to each person.

Although I gave Him little serious thought in my earliest years, I have no memory of life before God. Little kids are aware of the sun but don't pay much attention to anything but light and dark. Children accept the sun as a fact because it's there. God Dots were there from the beginning, but I wasn't taught to focus on the Dot Creator or to know Him intimately.

My grandfather was a Lutheran pastor serving as many as five tiny rural Midwest congregations at one time during the 1920s, '30s, and '40s. My earliest memories of him are as an invalid because his health began to deteriorate in the 1950s from Parkinson's and he passed away in January 1967. The more I learn about my grandfather, the more I wish I'd known him better because I have a feeling that we might have been kindred spirits. From stories I've heard and my own memories, my grandfather was different from my other relatives. His passion was farming, but when his eldest brother inherited the family farm, he had to find another way to earn a living. In addition to preaching, he also labored as a carpenter and handyman to feed his family. I believe my grandfather had a pure faith and a kind and generous heart.

My religious upbringing was routine for a mid-twentieth century kid, Sunday school, church, confirmation classes, and reciting grace before and after every family meal. I learned basic Bible stories, Lutheran liturgy and hymns, memorized weekly lessons from Luther's Catechism for three years (which I promptly forgot the next week), and prayed at the appropriate times. Many of the attributes Jesus taught to His disciples weren't alive in our home. My parents provided the basics of what I needed to live but fell short in the connection and love department.

THE GOD DOT

Which may explain why they never introduced me to the Person of God—the Dot Creator. Unless you know who God is, who Jesus Christ is, and who the Holy Spirit is, your God Dot map won't be of much use because you won't be able to distinguish a God Dot from coincidence or deception. Without an intimate relationship with the Dot Creator, you can't discern the truth when two preachers with big platforms or impressive credentials teach opposite lessons. Sometimes neither one is right. How can you know who to believe?

Distinguishing God from an Imposter

Is the graceful fish in the display aquarium at the exotic pet store a pacu or piranha? They look very much alike and share the same habitat, yet pacus are vegetarians while piranhas can strip a critter to its bones in less time than it takes to know that something is horribly wrong. If you put the new swimmer in the aquarium with your other fish, how can you know for sure whether he'll make friends or enjoy a quick snack? When food sources are scarce, piranhas happily eat one another.

Oddly enough, pacus aren't social creatures, abandoning their eggs to hatch, letting their offspring get along on their own. Piranhas, on the other hand, gather in groups and are quite the little social beasties. If there's a broad popular path for fish, piranhas are likely to be right in the middle, partying hearty while the peaceful pacus quietly swim off on the side without fanfare.

The most reliable way to tell a pacu from a piranha is by their teeth. Pacu teeth resemble human teeth while piranha choppers are more triangular. I don't know about you, but I don't plan to get friendly enough with either one to do a complete dental exam.

How much do you trust the clerk in the shop? If he hands you the peaceful pacu to take home but gets it wrong, the lives of your other fish are at stake. If you're willing to take his word that your pacu isn't a piranha, what inspires such trust? Sometimes knowledge is the difference between life and death. If you aren't a master ichthyologist, able to separate a gentle fish from a homicidal maniac just by looking, where do you get your information?

> My people are destroyed for lack of knowledge.
> —Hosea 4:6

> "Isaiah mourns in the same words, "Therefore my people are gone into captivity, because they have no knowledge" (Isaiah 5:13). They are destroyed for lack of it, for the true knowledge of God is the life of the soul, true life, eternal life, as our Saviour saith, 'This is life eternal, that they should know Thee, the only true God, and Jesus Christ whom Thou has sent.'"
>
> —Barnes Notes on the Bible

To recognize a genuine God Dot, you must know the Dot Creator.

If you saw the movie, *The Passion of the Christ,* you know that words cannot describe the graphic account of what Jesus willingly endured on your behalf. When people argue whether

Jesus is this or *Jesus is that*, the only way to know what to believe is to know who Jesus is—not who people say He is, but the truth. He is the man with shredded skin, blood flowing down His cheeks from thorn-puncture wounds, the man with open hands to receive iron spikes and who didn't resist when His ankles were nailed to a tree. Jesus is the man who entered Jerusalem knowing that His time was at hand and the Cross lay ahead, yet He walked in anyway.

What words describe Jesus's personality, attributes, and mannerisms? How much do you know about the character, heart, and love of God? When people tell you what God said in the Bible or interpret the verses and parables Jesus spoke, what's the best way to know if what they say is true? Learning to hear and recognize the voice of the Lord is a critical element of seeing and comprehending the markers He leaves for you.

Distinguishing God's Voice from the Competition

In his book, *Preparing Ourselves to Hear God's Voice*, Pastor Charles Morris, founder of Raising the Standard International Ministries, identifies five different voices that compete for your attention:

1. The voice within you
2. The voice of the world
3. The voice of lost religious leaders
4. The voice of the Enemy
5. The voice of God

Pastor Morris groups the voices that insist on self-concern and self-indulgence into four categories, numbers one through four on his list. The last voice, God's, is assaulted by the others, yet stands resolutely against them, immovable, imperturbable, and constant in volume. The voice of truth that belongs to God agrees with His Word, His character, His history, His promises, and asks you to lay down your life for Jesus, not stand on your rights, individuality, or opinions. All other voices lie, conspiring to separate you from God and prevent you from hearing His authentic voice by attempting to erode the underpinnings of your faith. Fear is a diabolical opportunist, marching in whenever faith falters.

GOD DOTS HAVE *no value unless you have a personal relationship with the Dot Creator.*

HOW DO you know if the voice you hear is God's, your own, or an imposter's? This is the crux of our dilemma today. You must know the source of the voice to know whether to listen or reject it. Unless you know the original source of what you hear, what you read, what you watch, or what you're taught, how do you know if it's true? Why do you believe what you do? More to the point, what you believe is powerless unless what you believe is real.

Have you ever heard from God? Do you receive through the Holy Spirit or rely on books, commentaries, videos, or online sermons from sober-minded, scholarly, or celebrity preachers? The source of inspiration is a critical component of any message and the only reliable source is God Himself.

How can you know if what you hear or read is reliable? Apply this test to every message.

God's voice:

- Always agrees with His Word.
- Perfectly represents His character.
- Conforms to His commands and promises.
- Always points to Himself.

The moment in the Garden of Eden when the serpent said to Adam and Eve, "Surely, God didn't say …," is the first time that deceit entered the world, tempting Eve to question what God said, a challenge every one of us still faces today. Never had man concerned himself about the identity of a speaker because there wasn't any competition. Ever since this event, recorded in the third chapter of Genesis, mankind has been inclined to reject submission and governance and has been unwilling to be shepherded. We prefer whatever soothes our itching ears over the daily work of pursuing relationship with God through Jesus Christ.

Imagine for a moment that you're unable to see the people you speak with. How do you know if they're who they say they are? A couple of years ago I answered a phone call and received this greeting, "Hi, Grandma."

"Well, hi—who is this?"

"Your grandson."

"Which one?"

"The oldest one."

"Ah. How are you? How's the family?"

"They're good and say hi."

"What's going on?"

"I'm in Atlanta for a friend's wedding."

I asked a few more questions, knowing that the caller was a scam artist and not one of our grandsons. His eventual sob story about getting arrested, his apology for embarrassing the family, and his pitiful request for bail money were thin enough to read through. But sometimes it's fun to let crooks paint themselves into a corner before calling them out. It didn't take long, and I disconnected.

How could I know it wasn't our grandson?

If someone told my husband that they overheard me telling a filthy joke or furiously demanding to speak to a manager in a store, he would tell them that they were mistaken because I don't do furious or off-color. How could he be so sure it wasn't me? Think of someone you know well enough to recognize by their footfall, scent, or special touch. Is there a voice you'd recognize anywhere in the world? Do you know what your spouse's mood is without asking?

Do you know the Dot Creator at least that well?

> *Therefore I speak to them in parables, because seeing they do not see, and hearing they do not hear, nor do they understand.* —Matthew 13:13

If you're confused or uncertain about your God Dot experiences, you're in good company. Everyone begins at the beginning. There were times when Jesus's teaching confused His disciples. He spoke in parables, behaved in ways they'd never seen before, and the content of His messages exceeded their ability to understand. Even simple parables were head-scratchers. Everyone reborn by the Spirit goes through the wine press and the refining fire of learning, becoming, and understanding.

How you experience the process is a personal matter between you and the Holy Spirit, but the elements remain largely the same and happen in roughly the same order. While it isn't the first step of sanctification, growing in knowledge, wisdom, and intimacy with the Lord is the step that requires your greatest focus, commitment, and obedience. Jesus was clear and consistent on this point—obedience. He was obedient to His Father, even unto death on the Cross.

> *If you love Me, keep My commandments.*
> —John 14:15

Two major motivations inspire obedience to the Lord. The first is fear, believing (rightfully) that you are a gnat before the blast furnace of God's authority and power. Wisdom begins with fear (Proverbs 1:7), but once you walk further with Jesus Christ, fear transforms into respect and awe becomes love.

The Dot Creator's Character

In the first three chapters of Genesis, the name of God changes three times. From Genesis 1:1 to 2:3, He is referred to as God

(Elohim), the Hebrew name for God. From there to the last verse of chapter three, He is referred to as the LORD God (YHWH Elohim), the Creator God. Beginning in the first verse of chapter four, He is called the LORD (YHWH), the covenant name for the God of Israel.

There was no other concept of God on the newly formed earth at creation so there was no reason to further define Him. Once there was a creation and created beings, His name changes to Creator God, defining His position relative to everything else. In chapter four there's a hint that things are about to change, and that God won't have the same relationship in the future with every created being or even every human.

Names in the Bible usually have meanings. For example, *Adam* is Hebrew for man, *Abraham* means the father of many, *Daniel* means God is my judge, *Elijah* means my God is Yahweh, *Isaac* means he will laugh, or he will rejoice, *Israel* means God contends, *Job* means persecuted, *John* means to be gracious, *Noah* means rest or repose, *Paul* means small or humble, *Satan* means adversary, and *Peter* means stone.

Most of these meanings suggest attributes or characteristics. Names are important to one's identity and individuality. Most people attach emotions or concepts to names. For example, when our first granddaughter was born, her parents named her Chloe. At the time I thought it an odd choice because the only Chloe I'd ever met was a beagle.

The names of God in the Bible introduce different aspects of His character, nature, and the way He interacts or touches our lives. In Chapter 7 you'll discover twelve types of God Dots.

The following sixteen names of God also hint at the ways He is active and present in your life.

Names of the Dot Creator

- Jehovah, "I AM WHO I AM." Exodus 3:13-15
- Jehovah-M'Kaddesh, the God who sanctifies. Exodus 31:13, Leviticus 20:7-8
- Jehovah-Jireh, the God who provides. Genesis 22:9-14
- Jehovah-Shalom, the God of peace. Judges 6:16-24
- Jehovah-Raah, the Lord my Shepherd. Psalm 23
- Jehovah-Rophe, the God who heals. Exodus 15:22-26
- Jehovah-Nissi, God our banner. Exodus 17:8-15, 1 Corinthians 15:57
- Jehovah Sabaoth, the Lord of hosts. 1 Samuel 1:3
- Jehovah-Shammah, the Lord is there. Ezekiel 48:35
- Jehovah-Tsidkenu, the Lord our Righteousness. Jeremiah 23:6
- El Shaddai, God Almighty. Genesis 17:1, 49:22-26
- El Elyon, the Most High God. Genesis 14:18
- El Olam, the Everlasting God. Genesis 21:33
- Adonai, Master or Lord. Genesis 15:2, 2 Samuel 7:18-20
- Elohim, Strength or Power. Genesis 1:1, Genesis 17:7-8
- Yahweh (YHWH), LORD or Jehovah. Genesis 2:4

IN 2008, my father and my stepmother dropped off some of my mother's things on their way home after a summer traveling by RV through the western United States. My mother passed away in 1995, and any newly discovered personal belongings were collected and passed along to me. The squat box contained a variety of her things, none of which I remember because of the one item that forever changed my relationship with Mother, even thirteen years after she died. Inside the cardboard time capsule were loose typewritten pages from her journal, dated when I was about fourteen.

God Dots arrive in every way imaginable, some wrapped in plain brown wrappers, their power hidden until you peel back the cover to view, digest, and react to their message. The first few pages I read were innocuous stream of consciousness notes about my father's spending habits and her decision to quit being concerned, accept the way things were, and live with it in peace. That was very much my mother.

Then the subject turned from her husband to her only daughter —me. My mother was a brilliant, respected, and active woman. A registered nurse, she was a natural take-charge type, chairing church committees, working in local political campaigns, sewing beautifully tailored clothes for herself, and making all my father's plans work out. She taught me to sew at an early age, expected my brother and me to be responsible and independent, and kept her opinions to herself. Once, when I was about the age of the journal notes I held in my hand, I remember being in the basement laundry room with her, holding a pair of hand-embroidered jeans that were all the rage in the 1960s. They didn't match her tailored and proper sense of style, so she threw them out whenever she got her hands on them, but I kept retrieving and wearing them. I embroidered them myself, stitching designs in various places, and applying a peace-symbol patch and a few others as decoration. Unlike denim fashion today, in the 60s anything with a threadbare spot became a rag or trash.

The incident is memorable because I asked for Mother's advice, which was a rare event. The subject wasn't anything unusual for a high school girl, but I remember being confused about the best way to handle something. She responded in her normal way, "I'm sure you'll figure it out." No opinion and no advice. I shrugged it off and decided not to waste my time asking again.

Reading further in her journal, I discovered a section where she tried to figure out a conundrum—me. Her tone and word choices read as if she were discussing a science project and I was the object under the microscope. On the neat pages I held in disbelief, my mother listed her observations, noting that although I was highly intelligent, my responses were unexpected, and that one explanation might be mental illness.

Her tapped-out words on decades old paper were dispassionate, deadpan, cold.

My father was my childhood nemesis, but I thought my mother perfect because she was immaculate, proper, matter of fact, unemotional, service-oriented, respected, and always under control. She served at church, as a Cub Scout pack leader, and as a nursing supervisor; she was a highly accomplished seamstress; she kept a neat home; and she budgeted down to the penny. One reason I placed her on a pedestal was because my father's behavior never pushed her off-script. No matter his outburst, tantrum, or fight with me, she remained cool and detached. Except once, which is the only time I ever saw her cry. Her quietly tearful response to yet another blow-up between her ten-year-old daughter and thirty-five-year-old husband was to slump (with perfect posture) into the corner of our Danish Modern living room sofa and whisper, "I can't choose between you." From an early age it was me against my father, until God worked it out decades later.

Still, I always assumed that she loved me and was dumbfounded when I read how she thought of me as she might a laboratory specimen, a bug. Since she was long gone there was no way to confront her. So, I did the next best thing. I walked outside, stood in the yard between the back of our house and the barn, raised the papers and my eyes to the sky, and confronted God. Even the little connection I felt to my mother was gone.

"Why didn't I have parents like other kids? I never had a father, and now I discover that I didn't have a mother either. What am I supposed to do with this?"

His reply was declarative, as if He thought I'd have figured it out after so many years and God Dots. This one ripped at my heart because I didn't understand it.

I never intended for you to have an earthly father because I am your Father. When were you ever alone? I was there before you recognized Me and there when you rebelled against Me. I've been there every moment and am here now and forever. You are Mine.

Psalm 27 is dear to my heart because it's my story with the Lord. The Holy Spirit brings us answers when we're able to process them and prepared to move on in the brilliant light of who God is to us and we are to Him.

> *The Lord is my light and my salvation;*
> *Whom shall I fear?*
> *The Lord is the strength of my life;*
> *Of whom shall I be afraid? (v. 1)*
>
> *When You said, "Seek My face,"*
> *My heart said to You, "Your face, Lord, I will seek."*
> *Do not hide Your face from me;*
> *Do not turn Your servant away in anger;*
> *You have been my help;*
> *Do not leave me nor forsake me,*
> *O God of my salvation.*
> *When my father and my mother forsake me,*
> *Then the Lord will take care of me. (vv. 8-10)*

THE GOD DOT I recorded that day redeemed every painful year in my past, revealed where I'd strayed, proved how the Lord always brought me back, and confirmed His plan for me. I knew the way forward and that I would walk it with Him every day without question, because He is my Father and I know He will never forsake me. God's relationship with each of His children is unique and nothing ever happens but that He's miles ahead of the outcome. If asked today if I'd like a different childhood, I'd answer without hesitation that I would not, because my childhood brought me to where I am today, and I wouldn't trade my relationship with the Lord for any precious childhood experience.

> *Lord, to whom shall we go? You have the words of eternal life.* —John 6:68

God Dots have a variety of purposes, but every time your Father makes His presence known is a gift of love that asks nothing but the same in return. Each day brings decisions ranging from insignificant to life altering. What direction should you take and with whom should you share the journey? Should you pull the kids out of school and begin teaching them at home? Should you save up for a different car or go into debt? Everything of value in life is either a stewardship issue or connected to a relationship. God Dots guide by warning, affirmation, and revelation. The closer your walk with Jesus Christ, the more God Dots you recognize and the more serenity and confidence you enjoy.

Somewhere along the way you realized that there is no other option besides Christ. You chose to listen, to study, and to walk in greater obedience because you know that you are insufficient in yourself. Eventually you come to crave private conversation and shared moments. God Dots reveal the presence, heart, faithfulness, and humor of God the Father, the Dot Creator.

> *"I go to prepare a place for you. And if I go and prepare a place for you, I will come again and receive you to Myself; that where I am, there you may be also. And where I go you know, and the way you know."*

THE GOD DOT

Thomas said to Him, "Lord, we do not know where You are going, and how can we know the way?"
Jesus said to him, "I am the way, the truth, and the life. No one comes to the Father except through Me."
—John 14:2-6

God Dot: *A glimmer into how much God loves us!* — Sandol Johnson

FIVE
THE DOTTED LINE

Enter by the narrow gate; for wide is the gate and broad is the way that leads to destruction, and there are many who go in by it.
Matthew 7:13

The quality, content, and direction of your life depends on where you are in relationship to God's vision and plan today. Are you on the narrow path God Dots define or on one of your own? If you're like many believers, answering that question isn't easy. It's normal to feel unbalanced or unsure when you don't know if you're going in the right direction.

"Are my feet where they belong?"

Driving in Texas the past few years, I've noticed that there are far fewer road signs. I can travel long distances without seeing a speed limit sign, and I feel vulnerable when I turn from a familiar highway onto an unfamiliar street or county road without a speed limit sign. Worrying about flashing red and blue lights closing in from behind isn't my happy place, especially if I could be technically guilty. Guessing the speed limit doesn't free me from concern that I won't get pulled over and go home with a ticket souvenir. I'm willing to obey the law, but how am I supposed to know what it is when there aren't any speed limit signs?

Sometimes other vehicles overtake and pass me, or I come up on cars that aren't moving along as fast as I am and realize with dismay that I'm speeding. Many times I've driven on a highway or road without seeing one speed limit sign before turning onto another road. It's nerve-wracking, wondering if you're doing it right, staying within the law, or breaking the law without the means to know right from wrong.

God Dots provide assurance, guidance, and confidence. No one feels secure when they don't know if they're on the right path or moving at the correct speed. Without markers of God's presence and the confidence of knowing you're in His will, insecurity begins to nibble away at the power you know is yours as a child of the King of Kings.

Common sense has little value when it comes to knowing God's plan and purpose for your life. Have you ever started toward a new destination by relying completely on GPS for directions? Maybe it's just me, but sometimes my GPS is loco. On one occasion, I was on a mix-master fly-over, more likely to run into a flock of geese than an intersection, when a dispassionate recorded voice told me to take an immediate right. I couldn't follow instructions without jumping the barrier and jettisoning a parachute I didn't have. I ignored the voice that we're supposed to trust.

God Dot.

Beware the sources you rely on for guidance.

The insecurity of not knowing where you are is huge, sapping your confidence, weighing on your spirit like a ball and chain, and sucking the life out of the boldness you owned yesterday. God Dots are the mile markers, street signs, and information billboards God provides to guide you to and keep you moving on the trail He blazed for you. Sometimes a God Dot arrives in the form of a highway helper when you're stuck. You don't know what to do because you broke down on a lonely stretch of highway, when suddenly a courtesy truck comes along that you didn't call. It stops, someone gets out and asks if you need assistance, and then provides whatever information or service you need to move forward or course correct.

When I look back at the line of Dots in my rearview mirror, I see many places where I wandered off track. Few things knock you off the path easier than temptation, and not always for something that people would consider wrong. The only way I knew I was sideways with God's plan for me is when I looked back and realized that the hard road I took wasn't the only choice. It seemed like the obvious move to my limited vision in the moment, but years later I recognized how many signs I missed or ignored. Yep, that happens, too.

On April 9, 1991, I welcomed a beautiful colt, Sky, into the world just after two a.m. He was amazing, gorgeous, and had more personality in his plush-coated little body than any of the hundred or so others I met at birth. When he was less than one day old, our veterinarian asked if he was for sale and how we'd price him. Dr. Madia's patients were almost exclusively show horses and he served all the top barns. He told me that most people wait a lifetime for a colt like this and never get it. Yet here I was, early in my horse career, and God delivered something special.

That's the moment I went off path, although I didn't realize it until eighteen years later. By then Sky had grown into a World and National champion and sired other World and National Champions. The final chapter of my book, *Amazing Grays, Amazing Grace*, is about Sky. When I sat down to write it, I believed that the bronze trophies gracing my office shelves were evidence of my greatest accomplishment. In that moment, tears pooled in my eyes and began to slow-roll down my cheeks because the Holy Spirit revealed that the bronzes weren't signs of success but witnesses to my tremendous failure.

I'd prayed for a horse to be my partner, confidant, and beloved family member from a time before I have memory. This colt was an answer to that prayer and I totally missed the sign. Instead of a personal gift from God, Sky became a teacher, challenge, and business asset. I knew he was special, and we bonded, but never in the way we might have if my feet had stayed on the dotted line God offered.

What I should have said was, "Lord, thank you. I recognize this wonderful gift and the answer to prayer you've given me," and then gone forward with the heart, the expectation, and the dream I'd cherished for decades — but I didn't. I'll never know how life would be different if I'd resisted the temptation to build a business around this special gift. I was an entrepreneur and said to myself, "Aha. I know how to leverage this." So, I did. It worked out well because God pivots to adjust the plan when you wander off course. The only reason I have the resume I do is because God had a plan for me, and it suited His purpose. He doesn't waste anything, not even our mistakes.

Everyone gets off track, some further than others, but God always knows precisely where you are and the nature of your circumstance. The bad news is that the further off track you get, the bigger the blow has to be to knock you back on. You may only need a gentle nudge if you're not that far off, but if you've strayed far away, the return trip may feel seismic or cataclysmic. The Holy Spirit will get as big and as obvious as needed for you to get the message. You have the choice to course-correct or quit His game altogether. I don't know what would have happened if I'd kept on the straight path back in 1991 because I didn't take it. But I will declare with total confidence that if your name is in the Lamb's Book of Life, God will bring you back. His plan and the finish line He has chosen for you never changes.

On Wednesday afternoons, I lead a Bible study for anyone who loves a deep dive into God's Word. We mine precious treasures of insight and relationship and then apply them to daily life. Our group began years ago as a mixture of pastors, business owners, faithful Bible students, and others who cycled in and out as schedules permit. Our oldest remaining member, nearing ninety as I write this, is an Invitation Machine. Much of his success as a lawyer and entrepreneur came from connecting with and inviting people to whatever he was doing.

In early March 2018, I walked into the conference room where our Bible study meets and greeted newcomer, Jon Dean (JD) Smith, a spry seventy-something gentleman who accepted an invitation to visit from the Machine. They'd known each other and their families for decades, crossing paths in church and business. We shook hands and exchanged quips about the Machine, because his unique sense of humor is a reliable icebreaker for anyone who knows his schtick. As we launched into robust consideration of Ecclesiastes, JD confidently and politely offered original observations or asked thoughtful questions in just the right places.

Engaged and substantive discussion of anything God-related is my happy place. I became more curious about JD as the hour wore on, particularly when I learned he'd written a book about discipleship. I don't remember who texted who first, but we decided to meet at a local McDonald's two days later for coffee. Ten minutes into our conversation I learned that JD was a speed-reader and had already finished three of my books. I replied that I'd also finished his, as I silently wondered where this was leading. JD's wife, Donna, suffered from advanced Parkinson's Disease and he was her primary caregiver. My husband and I met JD for lunch two weeks later. My next step was driving the twenty-five miles to their apartment to meet Donna. We scheduled a visit for the four of us the next week and the week after that.

In April, JD and Donna asked us to consider entering discipleship with them. For more than fifty years, JD planted churches, discipled others on an international level, pastored, taught, mentored other pastors, and wrote the manual on how to replicate discipleship the way Jesus taught. On the way home, my husband and I talked about the massive degree of commitment it would require, even though I didn't know what that would look like. It was a question of saying yes or no, not weighing pros and cons.

I wasn't surprised, because I'd recognized God Dots rushing into a straight line like iron shards to a magnet since the moment I met JD. Honestly, I didn't want to commit because I knew that accepting the invitation would open the door to some great unknown *more*. After years of building, investing, remodeling, pushing, learning, and doing what God called me to do, I was finally comfortable in my role as an author, in ministry, and with our horses. At that time, we lived in a barn I designed that delivered a lifelong dream while serving God and others. After years of growth and transitions I was ready to enjoy the delightful balance we finally achieved. Besides, neither of us was all that young, my husband only one year younger than seventy-eight-year-old JD.

My husband said he had to think about it. I immediately confessed that while I didn't want to, I knew that I had to accept. This God Dot wasn't a surprise, nor was it optional if I wanted to stay on the path God has for me. He never forces us to do anything, but being in His will is the sweetest place on earth and I wanted to stay there.

We both accepted. The four of us met twice a week to study, pray, and grow together. JD passed away from lung cancer just shy of our second anniversary. I'll share three more huge God Dots later in the book that made it abundantly clear that this was the path for us.

I'll share one more God Dot before moving on. JD, Donna, and I published a second edition of their book, now titled *The Hidden Truth*. The project took nearly a year, with JD's health declining so quickly in his last two months that I wondered if he'd see the project finished this side of eternity. But God's timing is perfect. I put a copy of the paperback into JD's hands four days before he entered hospice. His body ravaged by disease, but with an unquenchable spirit shining from his eyes, the picture of JD holding the book is one of my most precious memories. Later visits were short and powerful, and more about looking beyond the veil than any earthly project. In spirit, JD was already moving on to his next assignment.

God determines your transition into life and out of it. Remember the story about the dash on a tombstone? You have no say about the day you're born or the day you die, so the only material part of your story is what you do during the dash in between. There is a finish line set for you that serves God's purpose, moves the kingdom forward, and is ultimately all about Him. It may seem beyond imagination to think that God reserves a unique and material place for you in His plan, but He does. You're engaged for life once your feet settle onto your personal line of God Dots. You'll never be retired or pensioned off, and you will spend eternity in His presence, clothed in a mansion designed exclusively for you.

God Dots let you know that you're never alone, that your Father participates in even the smallest moments of life and knows you intimately, and they confirm that you're on track. Everyone must learn to recognize Dots and then train themselves to see them — it's not original equipment. The process of noticing and understanding God Dots is the path of sanctification, becoming closer to the Father, the Son, and the Spirit in each step.

God Dots illustrate and chronicle your walk with the Lord. He knows your name today and the new name you'll receive later. He knows your heart, your history, your present, and your future. The end of your dotted line is eternity in His loving presence.

God Dot: *Silent reassurance that He never leaves us.* — Kathryn McCrary

SIX
DOT DROUGHT

Ask, and it will be given to you; seek, and you will find; knock, and it will be opened to you. For everyone who asks receives, and he who seeks finds, and to him who knocks it will be opened.
Matthew 7:7-8

Sometimes God Dots seem to go on vacation leaving uncomfortable gaps in your map. A number of years ago, I shared rich private time with the Lord each morning. I enjoyed visits throughout the day and expected answers to my questions. The process of moving from being an entrepreneur to writing books and ministry was a time of deep conversation and intimate relationship with the Father. I did everything I was asked to do and grew into the role, relishing the close connection I had through the Holy Spirit. I thought more in terms of dialogue back then than God Dots. Being in the presence of God was more my norm than the exception.

Until it wasn't.

The morning of March 11, 2011, I awoke to a clear voice commanding me to "Tell them." Moments before I'd been dreaming and wasn't sure if the voice were speaking to the sleeping me or the wide awake me. It came again, "Tell them." I knew whose voice it was and asked what anyone would, "Tell them what?"

It was the morning of the tsunami and nuclear disaster at Fukushima, Japan. My husband watched the news as I tried to orient myself.

This is the end time. The King is coming. Choose today.

Eleven words. That's the message I was supposed to share. So far, my job was to say yes and do whatever I was asked to. It seemed reasonable to wonder who I was supposed to tell. I asked and received an answer just as I'd come to expect.

Write a book. The title is Rapture and Revelation. Tell them.

That's the sum of what I had to work with—eleven words and a title. After watching the horrendous news from Japan for over an hour, I padded to my office and sat down to write. Three hours and four thousand words later, I had a beginning.

Then I took a break.

And that's where I got off track.

The inner critic that we all harbor asked a few questions that seemed eminently reasonable in the moment. Who are you to write a book about rapture and revelation? You have nothing more than an eleven-word message. Why would anyone read anything you wrote on this subject?

Besides, I didn't have the right credentials, and that wasn't the kind of book that I write. Over the next weeks I tried moving the message forward but couldn't get a handle on it or rustle up the motivation to silence the naysayer who made good points. Maybe it was best to wait until God delivered a little more help.

And then I pretty much forgot about it.

When I think of that now it sounds ridiculous. How could anyone who receives a specific message and command from the Lord shove it to the bottom of her to-do pile like a recipe that sounded better yesterday? Imitating Scarlet O'Hara, I figured I would think about it again when it rose to the top or someone mentioned it. It wasn't my finest moment, but I haven't told you the worst part yet.

Months later, I sat with the Lord one morning and said, "I feel like we haven't been as close lately and our relationship is getting a little dry." I fully expected a conversational answer and that everything would be as it was because I showed up. The ministry was active, reaching people with our message and helping other gardeners to grow spiritual crops they'd already planted. Yet, the living water of inspiration was tasting a bit brackish and stale. I asked for fresh insight and guidance.

"What do you have for me to do?"

The answer wasn't the one I expected.

Do you remember that thing I asked you to do?

The message I shoved to the bottom of the pile suddenly took center stage.

"Yes."

Is it done yet?

"No."

Then what's your question?

I don't recall the rest of the conversation verbatim, but I think I may have whined a little.

"But I don't write books like this. I don't know how. And who am I to write about rapture and revelation?" As if God needed me to share a few facts He may have overlooked. There was no answer, but I got the message. I rummaged around and found the book file in my computer and started working again. And got stuck. And put it away again. It went to the bottom of the pile and I forgot about it. Again.

More months passed. The ministry was busy, but the day came when I asked again, "It's feeling kind of dry here, what would You have me do?"

You know that thing I asked you to do?

"Yes."

Is it done yet?

"No."

What's your question?

"Let me get this straight, am I to understand that until I write the book, we're pretty much done here?"

There was no further response, but I knew without a doubt that I'd understood the message perfectly.

I wrote the book.

It was hard because I lacked confidence in both the content and in my ability to do the work. Today I know that my mistake was thinking that I worked under my power when I was really working under His. I sent the manuscript to my editor with an abject apology because I thought it was a mess. Nothing else about that time remains in my short-term memory except this —the instant I tapped *send,* and the manuscript was on its way, the dam broke and spiritual water flowed like never before.

The book, *Rapture and Revelation,* is as much a lesson for me as it is for readers willing to take an honest look at why they believe what they do about God, faith, and what lies ahead.

God's patience is deeper than any trench in the ocean. Once you've tasted intimacy with Him it becomes as important to your survival as water and air, and maybe more.

God Dot: *A whisper from God.* — Nancy H.

SEVEN
TYPES OF GOD DOTS

One thing I have desired of the Lord, That will I seek:
That I may dwell in the house of the Lord All the days of my life, To behold the beauty of the Lord, And to inquire in His temple. For in the time of trouble He shall hide me in His pavilion;
In the secret place of His tabernacle He shall hide me;
He shall set me high upon a rock.
Psalm 27:4-5

God Dots mark the moments when the Lord steps out of heaven to establish, confirm, or obstruct your path. He makes Himself known to you in endlessly creative ways and for a variety of reasons. The types of God Dots I've encountered represent some of the ways He drops in to let you know He's there, whether you recognize it in the moment or decades after the fact.

Genuine God Dots are unexpected, always point back to the Dot Creator, and connect with other Dots on your map. Each one confirms faith in what is true or leads you to question that which is not.

12 Types of God Dots

1. Affection

Sometimes the God Dot arrives in the form of a spiritual bear hug so big I have to catch my breath. The message is, "I am here, and you are loved."

> *The Lord did not set His love on you nor choose you because you were more in number than any other people, for you were the least of all peoples; but because the Lord loves you, and because He would keep the oath which He swore to your fathers, the Lord has brought you out with a mighty hand, and redeemed you from the house of bondage, from the hand of Pharaoh king of Egypt.* —Deuteronomy 7:7-8

2. Affirmation

Yes, precisely. You're on the right path. Continue on. These God Dots may also confirm what you believe in the face of naysayers and detractors.

> *Then the Lord said to him, "Take your sandals off your feet, for the place where you stand is holy ground."* —Acts 7:33

> *While the earth remains,*
> *Seedtime and harvest,*
> *Cold and heat,*
> *Winter and summer,*
> *And day and night*
> *Shall not cease.* —Genesis 8:22

3. Assurance

God will correct, sustain, and protect you. "Be still, and know that I am God" (Psalm 46:10).

> *Yea, though I walk through the valley of the shadow of death, I will fear no evil; For You are with me; Your rod and Your staff, they comfort me.* —Psalm 23:4

> *Be strong and of good courage, do not fear nor be afraid of them; for the Lord your God, He is the One who goes with you. He will not leave you nor forsake you.* —Deuteronomy 31:6

4. Awareness

Notice this. Stop what you're doing so you can pay attention. Some God Dots appear to distract you from what you're concentrating on in order to draw your focus back to God, for a moment or for some larger purpose.

> *Behold, I send the Promise of My Father upon you; but tarry in the city of Jerusalem until you are endued with power from on high.* —Luke 24:49

> *For the vision is yet for an appointed time; But at the end it will speak, and it will not lie. Though it tarries, wait for it; Because it will surely come, it will not tarry.* —Habakkuk 2:3

> *Now therefore, listen to me, my children; Pay attention to the words of my mouth.*
> —Proverbs 7:24

5. Change of Seasons

Solomon wrote that everything has its season. God Dots announce or confirm that your season will change or has changed. Look forward with anticipation.

> *To everything there is a season, A time for every purpose under heaven.* —Ecclesiastes 3:1

Do not remember the former things,
Nor consider the things of old.
Behold, I will do a new thing,
Now it shall spring forth;
Shall you not know it?
I will even make a road in the wilderness
And rivers in the desert. —Isaiah 43:18-19

6. Discernment

Who is wise and who is the fool? Should you speak or remain quiet? Matthew 7:6 makes it clear that we must choose when to share our pearl of great price and when to protect its holiness from swine. Many times I've asked the Holy Spirit whether I should speak or remain silent.

Don't be surprised when a God Dot arrives in the very moment you wrestle with a dilemma of doing or not doing.

Behold, I send you out as sheep in the midst of wolves.
  Therefore be wise as serpents and harmless as
  doves. —Matthew 10:16

My son, if you receive my words,
And treasure my commands within you,
So that you incline your ear to wisdom,
And apply your heart to understanding;
Yes, if you cry out for discernment,
And lift up your voice for understanding,

> *If you seek her as silver,*
> *And search for her as for hidden treasures;*
> *Then you will understand the fear of the* L ORD *,*
> *And find the knowledge of God.* —Proverbs 2:1-5

7. Encouragement

Take heart, take one more step. You can, you will, and you are not alone. God Dots offer encouragement, offering simple help or support with tasks you find a bit overwhelming.

> *For whatever is born of God overcomes the world. And this is the victory that has overcome the world—our faith.* —1 John 5:4

> *"Have I not commanded you? Be strong and of good courage; do not be afraid, nor be dismayed, for the* L ORD *your God is with you wherever you go."* —Joshua 1:9

> *"Therefore I tell you, whatever you ask in prayer, believe that you have received it, and it will be yours."* —Mark 11:24

> *"These things I have spoken to you, that in Me you may have peace. In the world you will have tribulation; but be of good cheer, I have overcome the world."* —John 16:33

8. Guidance

Like breadcrumbs along the path, God marks the narrow road leading to eternity with Christ. These Dots mark the moments when you stop depending on your own abilities and let God lead. They encourage you to lean more on His understanding, wisdom, and power than your own.

These Dots may arrive as the answer to a known concern, like a surprise package.

I will instruct you and teach you in the way you should go; I will guide you with My eye.
—Psalm 32:8

Trust in the Lord with all your heart, and lean not on your own understanding; In all your ways acknowledge Him, and He shall direct your paths.
—Proverbs 3:5-6

Your ears shall hear a word behind you, saying, "This is the way, walk in it," Whenever you turn to the right hand or whenever you turn to the left. —Isaiah 30:21

9. Inspiration

These God Dots connect the unrelated, provide wisdom, and feed the creative soul.

> *Call to Me, and I will answer you, and show you great and mighty things, which you do not know.* — Jeremiah 33:3

> *And He has filled him with the Spirit of God, in wisdom and understanding, in knowledge and all manner of workmanship, to design artistic works, to work in gold and silver and bronze, in cutting jewels for setting, in carving wood, and to work in all manner of artistic workmanship.*
> *And He has put in his heart the ability to teach, in him and Aholiab the son of Ahisamach, of the tribe of Dan. He has filled them with skill to do all manner of work of the engraver and the designer and the tapestry maker, in blue, purple, and scarlet thread, and fine linen, and of the weaver—those who do every work and those who design artistic works.* — Exodus 35:31-35

10. Kindness

God Dots frequently come when you need a spiritual hug or a convenient parking place. They can provide for a need you haven't yet voiced, like a coffee shop you've never seen before that pops up at the very moment you need refreshment.

God Dots: *Kisses from heaven.* — Tania Leanne Earle

But when the kindness and the love of God our Savior toward man appeared, not by works of righteousness which we have done, but according to His mercy He saved us, through the washing of regeneration and renewing of the Holy Spirit. — Titus 3:4-5

How precious is Your lovingkindness, O God! Therefore the children of men put their trust under the shadow of Your wings. —Psalm 36:7

Because Your loving kindness is better than life, my lips shall praise You. —Psalm 63:3

11. Revelation

God Dots are unexpected, point back to the Dot Creator, and are linked with something bigger than a moment. For example, an eleven-word message that wakes you up with instruction to share it. Years later, I recognized that it was a seed waiting for connection to future Dots. Then overnight it shot up like the plant God provided Jonah.

And the Lord God prepared a plant and made it come up over Jonah, that it might be shade for his head to

> *deliver him from his misery. So Jonah was very grateful for the plant.*—Jonah 4:10

> *After these things I looked, and behold, a door standing open in heaven. And the first voice which I heard was like a trumpet speaking with me, saying, "Come up here, and I will show you things which must take place after this."*—Revelation 4:1

12. Warning

God Dots also provide cautionary signals. No. Not that way, not that person, not this time. Turn around.

> *And the woman said to the serpent, "We may eat the fruit of the trees of the garden; but of the fruit of the tree which is in the midst of the garden, God has said, 'You shall not eat it, nor shall you touch it, lest you die.'"* —Genesis 3:2-3

> *Now when they had departed, behold, an angel of the Lord appeared to Joseph in a dream, saying, "Arise, take the young Child and His mother, flee to Egypt, and stay there until I bring you word; for Herod will seek the young Child to destroy Him."* — Matthew 2:13

THE GOD DOT

Then Isaac called Jacob and blessed him, and charged him, and said to him: "You shall not take a wife from the daughters of Canaan." —Genesis 28:1

Let your eyes look straight ahead,
And your eyelids look right before you.
Ponder the path of your feet,
And let all your ways be established.
Do not turn to the right or the left;
Remove your foot from evil. —Proverbs 4:25-27

YOU'LL SEE many God Dots in the rearview mirror, evidence of God's presence in your life in earlier days. I've experienced God Dots spotlighting my horrible choices or failures from the past and how they fit into my dotted line. Out of kindness, mercy, and grace, God brings them to your awareness years after the fact when the revelation brings understanding and connection instead of intense and abject shame. The Lord is too loving and kind to twist the knife in an open wound. He waits until the offense is long past, the injury healed, or the scab thick enough to show you how deep and ugly it was without damaging your confidence, hope, and purpose.

What I learn when past God Dots reveal themselves is that, while the error or injury caused was my own doing, God took the hit instead of me. He is the Master of perfect timing and kindness, waiting to reveal how certain Dots connect until you're able to receive the news in a way that affirms and strengthens your faith.

LYNN BABER

A God Dot to me is a gentle reminder (usually occurring just when I need it most) that I matter to Him. That He cares and He is near, even when I don't feel like He is. — Janet Holt Craig

EIGHT
THE FAITH GAP

And Jesus said, "For judgment I have come into this world, that those who do not see may see, and that those who see may be made blind."
John 9:39

The Faith Gap is the interval between fixed God Dots, the places where you know God is present in your life or has reached out to share an intimate moment with you, His beloved child. Faith Gaps come in two broad categories: at times of rebellion, delusion, or lack of awareness, or times of quiet when the Holy Spirit doesn't speak. Even so, you walk without fear, remaining confidently in the center of God's will because your faith is strong enough to withstand times of trials and periods of quiet.

The most precious saints in history knew that silence from God was often proof that they walked in perfect obedience. Faith matures by discovering that every test includes a place of perfect peace and release, but you must actively seek it out. God establishes the circumstances then patiently watches your struggle to find freedom from turmoil. Learning that God does work everything together for our good is critical to developing boldness and growth. I used the same process to teach horses to seek and find the place of total freedom I built into every situation. Eventually, some had greater faith in me than in their natural sense of self-preservation. Building trust begins by applying a small bit of pressure. No one likes feeling trapped or in a bind, no matter how slight. The first time the horse moved all or part of its body and discovered that it had the power to eliminate the bind, the dance of faith began.

Horses learned to seek the place of release because I made certain that it was always present and discoverable. When a horse is *in my will*, it's free from direction, restraint, pressure, or concern. My relationship with some horses made it possible to communicate in ways so subtle that others couldn't see them. The horse appeared to move in perfect peace and freedom because there was nothing for me to correct or refine. The more we communed by invisible means, the fewer verbal or touch messages needed to assure the horse that it was still doing everything I hoped for. Those moments are precious.

Learning to walk with the Lord works the same way. It's not so much about triumph and power as it is tranquility of spirit. Like a hot air balloon riding air currents, being in God's will is going with the flow—no struggle, no friction, and no ragged edges. These moments between visible God Dots prove that He trusts you to walk without supervision. When you are in His will there is no bind, no pressure, no sense of limitation, and perfect peace.

Many God Dots on my personal map weren't visible until many years after the fact. A soul-wrenching breakup with my first fiancé was the most painful period in my life. He was the only person who ever stood up to my father on my behalf and loved me for who I was, a massive first in my experience. We planned a life together, named three future children, and the only earthly witnesses at his baptism were the pastor and me. But the relationship couldn't withstand the pressures of two young people struggling to find their way with few resources and no support system, even though our connection was real and lasted for many years after we last saw one another. I couldn't understand how a loving God that I knew and honored could do this to me. He brought us together, was part of something rare, and then allowed it to end.

I didn't believe there was one piece of my shattered heart big enough to move forward. Once I knew that I wasn't going to die, I became angry, blaming God for what I considered betrayal, lies, and leading me on. Did my pain amuse Him? He listened to my whispered screams, watched me cry a lifetime of tears, and offered no response when I told Him in specific terms that if this was the way He did things, I wanted no part of it. We were done. I didn't blame my fiancé then and still don't. I blamed God. That, however, has changed.

For years, that break up was a God Dot hidden by a thick scab of hurt and confusion. Like a bird gaining strength with every peck at the egg separating it from the outside world, the struggle gave me strength. That relationship didn't end because God had abandoned me, but because He'd claimed me years earlier and was faithful to keep me from wandering too far off the path leading to His vision and purpose for my life. If I had the opportunity to choose between my fiancé and God back then, God wouldn't have stood a chance.

Which, I realized later, was precisely why the relationship ended.

In the rearview mirror I understood that the experience was a huge God Dot, because it taught me that I was lovable. But in the moment and the following years, it was pure pain. Even so, I was always grateful that I'd known such love even if it never came again. Recognizing God's willingness to watch me suffer, tolerate the blame I sent His way, and endure my thankless tirades was another magnificent God Dot I added to my map thirty years later.

Faith gaps are the places between God Dots, spaces where you aren't aware of God's active participation in your life. The gaps occur when Dots go unnoticed and unseen, whether from distraction, a lack of awareness, rebellion, or insufficient faith. I missed the Dots related to my first fiancé nearly fifty years ago for a combination of those reasons. I'm sharing this because I want you to know that while God may seem like an unkind father, He is not. He is patient, kind, and willing to shoulder harsh accusations from His beloved children when caused by brokenness He has yet to repair. God can and will fully restore whatever damaged thing you place before Him with extravagance and endless love.

"God is too good to be unkind and He is too wise to be mistaken. And when we cannot trace His hand, we must trust His heart." —Charles Spurgeon

MY ANGER against God was a necessary part of learning who He is. Too few pastors teach their congregants about the nature and heart of the Father, the Son, and the Holy Spirit. Folks with a few years of Sunday school under their belts know that true Christianity is a relationship, not a religion. It's not about the way you share your faith with others, but the shared love of a Person who loved us first. If my faith in God's character had been stronger than the heartbreak of broken love, the aftermath would have been far easier. But, like everyone else, I learned by experience.

Who is the true father, the man who walked out on his natural children and their mother, or the man who made an unbreakable commitment to love, support, and be there through good times and bad? The man who sacrificed himself to provide and love, dry tears of hurt, and share tears of joy, but whose name isn't on any birth certificate?

The refining fire of your walk with Christ is real, designed to expose hidden impurities of faith and transform remnants of fear and doubt into a precious, pure confidence in Jesus Christ. The further into the flame you move, the more power you receive as a New Creation in Christ through the Holy Spirit. The hotter the flame the brighter the faith. God knows you better than you know yourself, which is why He gives you space to move forward on your own. The Dot Creator is a provider, not a crutch. He wants you to understand the depth of your own ability to walk His vision toward the finish line and victory.

> *And we have known and believed the love that God has for us. God is love, and he who abides in love abides in God, and God in him. Love has been perfected among us in this: that we may have boldness in the day of judgment; because as He is, so are we in this world. There is no fear in love; but perfect love casts out fear, because fear involves torment. But he who fears has not been made perfect in love. We love Him because He first loved us.* —1 John 4:16-19

God's plan for you is washed in love through the blood of Jesus Christ. He abides in you and empowers you to be bold in this world as well as the next. Torment comes from fear and the father of lies, not from the good Father who is ever present, always cares, and will move even the stars of heaven to deliver you into His presence once He claims you as His child.

Consider the parable of the prodigal son in Luke 15:11-32. The young man wasn't content at home with Dad. He was flooded with impatience and demanded his inheritance so that he could do things his own way and be the master of his destiny. Once he wasted his fortune on meaningless pleasures, he found himself homeless and hungry, envious of the swine with a cozy pigsty for shelter and plenty to eat. With nothing left to lose, he headed for home, finally aware that any station in his father's house was more blessed than where he was.

If the date the youngest son left was one God Dot and the date his father welcomed him home with open arms another Dot, the time in between could be considered a Faith Gap. The problem was the young man, not his father. The father provided everything his son needed, from love to a secure and bountiful future, but the boy rejected it for independence. The urge to indulge himself was greater than regard for his father. When that plan tanked, he returned home to face any consequence imposed.

His father never wavered in loving his son, didn't move without leaving a forwarding address, never rejected him or changed the locks, and waited until the boy found his way home. The time gap, the difficult road, the lure of bright lights that burnt swiftly out, and the dismal place the prodigal son found himself were the fruit of his choice. The Faith Gap was in the son's heart, not in his father's constancy, love, and provision.

Let's step above the parable for a moment and remember that coincidences don't exist. Whether we know it or not, everything happens in its season and proper order. I don't mean that everything is fixed, that every event is preordained, or that we're nothing but robots on a leash. But God sees all, knows all, is never surprised, and has Plan B ready before we recognize Plan A. Everything, regardless of your detour or bad decision will ultimately turn out for your good (Romans 8:28).

Imagine for a moment that you are the prodigal son, and the father is your Heavenly Father. You are free to take every blessing He's given you and strike out on your own, rejecting His authority, His plan, and His presence. But if your name is in the Lamb's Book of Life there's only one ultimate result—eternity with Jesus Christ. The immediate issue is getting you back home.

So, life gets tough. Things don't work out the way you want them to and the pickle grows sourer by the day. Then one day you look around and realize with searing shame that you are the fool. Not only are you serving swine, but their standard of living is higher than your own. (My apologies to swine. I happen to love pigs.) Once you get your head out of the mire, you remember that even the lowest of the low in your Father's house have it pretty sweet. The way back is through the gate of repentance, which is a small price to pay to return to the warmth, security, and benevolence of a Father who never lost His vision for your life.

Who had a hand in creating your tough experience? Certainly, every choice the son made was horrible, but did he come to serve hogs by coincidence? Add another God Dot to his map.

Struggles build strength and motivate you to seek something different or better. No one seeks rescue if they're sitting pretty where they are. Who seeks a savior unless they need one? There's no reason to rock the boat if you're content and comfortable. But if your boat begins to take on water and the level of sea water outside is close to the level of water inside your boat, who do you want sitting beside you?

Even when you don't recognize the Teacher's hand, your lessons continue. On some future day, a celestial spotlight will illuminate your past experiences to reveal how everything to date lines up in common purpose. This is your line of God Dots, each event interwoven with all others, like a cord of three strands—purposeful and unbreakable (Ecclesiastes 4:12).

The line of God's unique purpose for you isn't a series of random points (Dots) separated by long periods of time, even if it seems that way today. The space or interval between the moments of awareness when God is powerfully and intimately present in your life is a Faith Gap. The greater your awareness and confidence in the Father, and the more you see Him in action, the smaller the space between the God Dots on the map of your personal journey become.

If you're in the midst of a Faith Gap, what do you think is the reason? Are you listening to the wrong voices, rebelling against God's will, or are you in that blessed place of perfect peace and release?

God Dots: *Connect the Dots with the one who makes the dots.* — Barbara Clinkscales

NINE
ENEMIES: FAITH AND FEAR

I sought the Lord, and He heard me, And delivered me from all my fears. They looked to Him and were radiant. And their faces were not ashamed.
Psalm 34:4-5

No matter who you are, where you are, how old you are, or your circumstance today, God is willing to reveal Himself to you. You already know that God is endlessly creative and employs whatever means is needed to connect. Some God Dots are glorious while others are the opposite of anything you expected or were prepared for.

Some God Dots arrive in attractive packages with hidden features waiting to surprise you in challenging ways. I wouldn't have written that a few years ago, but I know better now because one of my God Dots is Journey, an Appaloosa gelding we rescued from a kill pen. His photo on a social media rescue site almost jumped off the screen when I saw it. How do you describe that special something, an inexplicable connection with someone or something you've never met? The last thing we needed was another horse because we had just celebrated my sixtieth birthday and my husband's seventy-fourth. At that point, downsizing sounded smarter than upsizing and we had more than enough horses to be well mounted for the rest of our lives. After mentioning the Appaloosa to my husband and getting a less-than-enthusiastic response, I tried to forget about him.

In case you didn't know, I was an equine professional for thirty years, specializing in training and showing stallions for many of them. I worked with special-needs horses for ten years, earning the confidence to deal with almost any horse issue. My teachers were wild horses, emotionally broken horses, unbalanced horses, aggressive horses, hopeless horses, stubborn horses, and spoiled, fearless horses. One God Dot that reveals how the Lord knows me better than I know myself arrived minutes before the Appaloosa gelding was about to ship to Mexico for a horrific end. I walked into my husband's office and said, "You know that Appy gelding I showed you a week ago? He ships in less than an hour. What do you think?"

I wanted a Get-Out-of-Guilt-Trip-Free card and expected my very intelligent husband to tell me what I wanted to hear. "We don't need any more horses. No!" But that's not what he said. He crossed his arms, silently looked down at his chest longer than made me comfortable, then replied, "I think you better try and buy him."

THE GOD DOT

Gulp.

In that instant, a shadow crossed over my spirit because this wasn't my first God Dot rodeo. I knew that this was bigger than just saving a horse, but I was still blissfully unaware of what I was getting myself into. So, I bought Journey, knowing nothing more than what part of the right side of his body looked like. Remember how I owned my confidence, especially when it came to horses? Fear didn't live in my house. My early life was nine bushels of tribulation and a thousand miles of hard road, but God brought me through all of it. I was a survivor and on the far side of the battle—or so I thought.

The Appaloosa gelding's basic personality was kind and he seemed willing enough, although curiously reactive in certain situations. Looking back, I realize that he had an early *tell*, something that should have clued me in to deeper trouble, warning me of what was coming. If I were still in the business, I'd never forget the way Journey appeared to bolt without moving his feet, and I'd recognize it if I ever saw it again. I've worked with some powerfully difficult horses, but this guy was the most dangerous one I've met because his explosive center was wrapped in an intelligent reasonable cover.

Whoever tried to "break" him did, but not to ride, and I knew why he'd been thrown away. Someone broke through his emotional ceiling by pushing him past the point that he could manage his fear. When he rocketed into panic, he entered an internal cosmos of terror severing his connection to earth and me. Normal people and animals learn to manage stress, uncertainty, and even tolerate high levels of pain. But once the emotional ceiling fails from abuse or unmanageable fear, the psyche has to leave the building or die.

I understand the phenomena. During an evening Christmas service when I was about nine, I stood in the front row wearing my maroon junior choir robe and ivory stole. My next memory is waking up in a dark stairway with my mother and someone else beside me asking me if I was okay. Over the next sixteen years I blacked out a handful of other times for no apparent reason. Were they faints or quiet seizures? After numerous EEGs and other diagnostic testing when I was twenty, my doctor explained that it was stress. When stress exceeded my capacity to process it, my brain simply shut down.

I understood why my rescue horse did what he did, but that didn't make it any less dangerous. After a few months of trial, error, progress, and regress with Journey, I met with the Lord one morning as I always do.

"Lord, I don't want to do this. I know how to work with this horse—but I don't want to. I'm too old."

He waited.

"And besides, I'm afraid."

I don't know if it was an admission or a confession. The next thing I asked for was a pass, to be released from the assignment. No pass came and I knew I had to finish the job, whatever it took and wherever it led. Looking back, I appreciate how God was too faithful to let me walk away covered in the stain of fear. Faith and fear never share the same space, which meant that there were places left in my spirit still ruled by fear. God knows us way better than we know ourselves.

THE GOD DOT

You can't escape God. He's everywhere and endlessly patient, but you can't outsmart Him, outlast Him, out stubborn Him, or outrun Him. You can delay, resist, rebel, and ignore, but one day you realize that the only reasonable response is yes.

God is faithful to provide a pathway to faith stronger than any fear, but it's up to you to walk it. There were three possible outcomes with the gelding: he would come along–and all would be well—he'd kill me, or I'd end up physically broken. I already had metal in both feet, one wrist, and a spiffy titanium knee. Getting killed isn't as big of a deal to me as the getting busted part. Once I accepted that this was a direct assignment from the Lord, I stepped out in faith.

Nevertheless, not my will, but Thine be done.

Three months later I was riding the gelding. Three years later I loved Journey and trusted him. Every lesson began with the three of us in prayer because I never wanted to ride alone. It was always the gelding, me, and the Holy Spirit. Fear never leaves willingly—faith must evict it. Christian fear is rooted in one of two concerns, that God isn't powerful enough to handle your problem or that He won't handle it the way you want Him to.

What are you afraid of? What prevents you from seeing God Dots all around you? Are you in denial, full of doubt, fearful, distracted, or unwilling? The God Dot journey is a faith walk that requires open eyes, a trusting heart, and a spirit sensitive to what's around you. God Dots shine a light on your past and look into the future.

Will you walk the dotted line God created exclusively for you? If you do, He'll empower you to dream dreams, see visions, and serve as His hands and feet on earth by establishing faith that annihilates fear.

God Dots: *Blessings from the Father!* — Deb B.

TEN
GENUINE DOTS

And Joshua said to them, "Cross over before the ark of the Lord your God into the midst of the Jordan, and each one of you take up a stone on his shoulder, according to the number of the tribes of the children of Israel, that this may be a sign among you when your children ask in time to come, saying, 'What do these stones mean to you?' Then you shall answer them that the waters of the Jordan were cut off before the ark of the covenant of the Lord; when it crossed over the Jordan, the waters of the Jordan were cut off. And these stones shall be for a memorial to the children of Israel forever."
Joshua 4:5-7

The one thing every genuine God Dot has in common is that it points directly to the Dot Creator. Any event, sign, or feeling that puts anything or anyone else on center stage is an imposter dot, not a personal message from the Dot Creator. Another characteristic of God Dots is that they're unexpected.

In the early 1990s, my business grew as I earned recognition as a horse breeder, trainer, and judge. There were amazing God Dots that I didn't appreciate until years later, some of which came with the burdensome weight of mounting tragedies and loss, especially in the breeding side of the business.

Losing a competition can be disappointing, but I consider that kind of failure a fabulous opportunity to course-correct, refine, and return the next time more precisely prepared to win. Getting beat is part of the learning curve. Losing a foal, a newborn horse, is devastating enough one time, but we hit a stretch where we lost several in a very short period. Worse, we lost the remarkable ones who arrived with obvious star quality. All our foals were the product of champions, but some just had that special something, that "it"—whatever that is.

Each circumstance was different and there was nothing we could have done to prevent even one heart-wrenching loss. The vet bills were staggering, but the most devastating cost was emotional, because each foal represented more than a year of preparation, care, investment, and sweet dreams for the future. We did everything possible to save each soft, beautiful baby, his mama standing silently by, hoping her foal would bump her to nurse again and that everything would be okay. I remember watching tiny ribcages lift and settle, knowing that every passing minute depleted a life force that was too young to have any reserve.

Within a few weeks, because of veterinarians who failed to communicate with each other, we unnecessarily lost Oreo, a gorgeous two-day-old colt I knew would be a future champion. We lost Licorice, a thirty-day-old coal black colt with a brilliant white star and one flashy hind stocking. I'd already claimed him as my forever horse. One morning I walked through the barn as usual, but Licorice didn't bound over to greet me. He lay quietly in the corner of the stall in no obvious distress while his mother ate her breakfast—but this wasn't normal. I called the vet at once and told him that Licorice was colicking.

"Babies that age don't colic."

The vet was sure I had the diagnosis wrong but knew that something was up. But I didn't have it wrong. Licorice came through a surgical resection like a champ, but his digestive system never woke up, forcing me to give permission to put him down just a few hours after I'd visited him in the clinic where he'd been alert and bright, demanding my attention in his insistent impish way—but also about to fail.

The final straw was the loss of a three-week-old colt with a once-in-a-lifetime combination of pedigree, pizazz, and conformation. In the middle of a high Sonoran Desert spring afternoon, a friend and I lay on the colt's body, she across his hip while I held his shoulder down to prevent him from struggling to get up on a shattered right foreleg. Sometimes God gets dramatic when He wants to make a point. Dark clouds roiled in the western sky as if called by a malevolent force. The wind cooled then began to blow in earnest. We lay across the colt, dried manure dust and sand stinging our eyes, waiting for the vet to arrive, praying we could save the soft, storybook baby sheltered beneath us. After a quick look, the vet told me there was only a fifteen-percent chance the colt would ever be breeding sound and zero that he'd be able to walk normally. I let him go. His registration papers arrived the day he died.

There's far more to tell than the loss of these three colts in quick succession, but I've shared enough to make the point. I got tired of hearing people say, "If it wasn't for bad luck, you'd have no luck at all." There was nothing we could fix, change, or improve because we'd done everything right.

The night we lost the last colt, I was done and out of try. Knowledge, ability, and experience weren't good enough or powerful enough to fix whatever was wrong. I gave up the battle. I sank to my knees in my closet and laid everything at the foot of the Cross. There was nothing left in me. "I'm tapped out. Done. Finished. I got nothing left." Which is exactly where God wanted me. I admitted that I didn't have the strength to walk the path He had for me under my own power. Tomorrow, and every day thereafter, would be on His terms, under His plan, His protection, and His guidance. *My* business was finished. That night I quit thinking about what I did, believing that I had the power to make anything happen, and gave everything to the Lord. If He took all the babies, then so be it.

> "Thank God for the sight of all you have never yet been. You have had the vision, but you are not there yet by any means. It's when we are in the valley, where we prove whether we will be the choice ones, that most of us turn back. We are not quite prepared for the blows which must come if we are going to be turned into the shape of the vision. We have seen what we are not, and

what God wants us to be, but are we willing to have the vision "batter'd to shape and use" by God? The batterings always come in commonplace ways and through commonplace people." — Oswald Chambers (*My Utmost for His Highest*, 10/3)

We never lost another foal, and our successes began to mount. I never forgot who made that happen. I was successful because God has a plan for me and He has one for you, too. I didn't recognize the extravagance of this God Dot until I looked back and saw how He connected it to what went before and after.

Some might look at the heartbreak we endured and blame the Enemy. Whether God orchestrated or permitted our losses, I know that the aftermath of surrender is worth everything it took to get me there. Genuine God Dots produce strength, peace, and resolve, and they destroy fear. I don't want to give you the impression that we never faced challenges or loss again. God Dots continued to come over the years, but in the rearview mirror, losing that last foal was one of the biggest.

I'M willing to do whatever God has in mind and give everything to Him because it's His anyway. Other major God Dots arrive in the moments when I fail to see His plan, remember a message, or move too quickly. Remember my rescue horse, Journey? God used him to deliver two huge Dots, one I mentioned in my lesson about fear and the second as the result of forgetting an agreement with God. It still mystifies me that it's possible to forget something God said that I clearly understood and intended to do.

In late summer 2018, Journey was one of my two favorite horses. I had big plans for us, but God made it clear that Journey wasn't the forever horse I thought he was and that God had another home for him. The message came through loud and clear, "Get Journey ready and I'll send someone for him."

No one else had ever saddled or ridden him so I didn't know if he was really trained or if he was a one-woman pony. Getting him ready meant finding that out. I called a horse savvy friend to ask if she'd work with Journey for a month because I knew she wouldn't hurt him, and he wouldn't hurt her. He was a handful for the first week, but then settled in and made it clear that he loved woods and trails. She liked him and her husband wanted to keep him, but it wasn't the home I knew God had in mind, so Journey came home.

Did I tell you how much I liked him? I loved how responsive he was to me, the way he looked and moved, and he fit me perfectly. Sitting on him felt like home. He hadn't been back from my friend's for even a few days when I fell in love with him all over again and promptly forgot what God had said, that Journey wasn't mine and that He would send someone else for him.

Have you ever repeated a mistake? The circumstances aren't the same, but the underlying error is. I hate that, and appreciate God's patience, which only lasts so long. Months passed, winter blew in, and I had a new book launching soon. The horses didn't get as much work as usual, spending more time as a herd than as my partners. On May 2, 2019, I came home after a long day and felt the need to get on a horse the way some folks say they need a drink. I pulled Journey from his stall, tossed a dressage saddle on his back, and we walked out to the small, covered pen on the west end of the barn we lived in. I didn't intend to work, thinking more about sharing a moment with one of my favorite "people" than anything else.

Standing in the center of the pen, I let Journey stretch before mounting since I hadn't ridden him in a while. I asked him to walk around the arena perimeter once or twice and step over four ground poles arranged on the north wall. He was obedient as expected, so I asked him to go the other way at a walk and then once around at a trot. After I stepped onto the mounting block in the corner, Journey walked over. I could walk seventy-five feet away from him, stand on a mounting block looking in the opposite direction, and he'd walk over in a straight line, take one lap around the block, and stop so the stirrup was next to my foot.

Here's one admission I've never made before—Journey fed my ego because he offered to do things for me no other horse ever had. He worked at liberty without a halter or rope at any gait, going faster or slower, changing direction, and never leaving a perfect circle around me, whether large or small, just by obeying my breath commands. No cues or gestures, just changes in my thoughts, energy, and breathing.

Journey was relaxed when I got in the saddle and we walked off. We rode around the pen once and then over the ground poles. Crossing the center of the arena my world suddenly went sideways. One moment Journey was walking flat and loose and the next I hit the ground. Hard. You can't imagine how badly I want just a two-second video of the moment to see what happened. It made no sense, but I knew I messed up somewhere. In hindsight, I don't know how I got up, but I did and shuffled over to where Journey stared at me from one corner as if I were a ghost. I knew I was hurt, but I wouldn't leave him wearing a bridle and bit. After opening the arena gate (a miracle in itself), I led Journey to his stall, pulled the bridle, and then walked to the door between the horse side of the barn and the house side. I couldn't turn the handle, so used some part of my body to press the doorbell and waited for my husband to answer.

I separated one shoulder, sprained the other, sprained a wrist that would have broken but for the titanium plate and nine screws already in it, and had a mild concussion. I couldn't lift a piece of paper with either hand. This was a God Dot. I knew it, understood it, and felt like a wretch because I'd failed both God and Journey. The way I explain what happened is that an angel, the Holy Spirit, or other agent of the Lord reached down, touched Journey, and I hit the dust. It wasn't about the horse, but that I'd forgotten what God told me the previous summer.

Journey wasn't mine, but I'd kept him and continued to make plans for our future. I didn't refuse or disobey intentionally, I just plumb forgot. Then I had another concern. Did I mess up the plan? Would the person God intended to have Journey still come? That ship had sailed, but I was assured that God would still send someone. He did, and in a way that became an entire God Dot bouquet.

Four hours after I learned that another clinician I trusted and admired was interested in Journey, he was on his way to a new home and adventure in another part of Texas. The deal was sealed when she pulled back her shirt sleeve to show me a silver bracelet.

"I didn't know why I was led to start wearing this a month ago, but now I do."

The bracelet was engraved with one word, Journey.

Even when we aren't faithful, He is.

Genuine Dots always point to God as He is— loving, balanced, faithful, creative, and with a vision and plan that He intends for you to achieve. When you fail to understand, lose your way, or outright forget what He said, He is faithful to do whatever it takes to get you back on the correct Dot Line.

God Dots are unexpected and always connect to others. If your Dots don't form an intelligible picture yet, don't be discouraged. The first God Dot is the beginning of an amazing journey. Every successive Dot is another gift proving that God is always with you and adds to the others to create a map designed just for you.

God Dots: *I've always thought of them as His whispers to my soul.* — B. Stasser

ELEVEN

DOT BLINDNESS

For you were once darkness, but now you are light in the Lord. Walk as children of light.
Ephesians 5:8

Dot Blindness comes in two varieties: Dots you miss, and Dots you convince yourself aren't there. In 1977, three weeks after the first Star Wars movie was released, and two days before my first wedding, I walked along rural roads partitioning vast crop fields into one-mile-square sections southwest of Omaha, Nebraska. I'd been a resident of the state for all of one week after packing up and moving from Minneapolis ahead of schedule because my fiancé was injured at work, and I wanted to fly to his side. He wasn't badly hurt, but young love is often impulsive. We stayed with my prospective in-laws until pronounced man and wife by a local judge with my future brother- and sister-in-law as witnesses.

A fat, neon-lit God Dot accompanied me on my solitary walk. I have no excuse for missing it because the sky was clear with sunshine and a delightful breeze blessed the corn and soybean fields around me. My mind and heart were unsettled, and I wondered if the shadow I felt over me was anything more than the product of an overactive imagination.

Memory is a swirling eddy, combining what we accurately remember with bits that we hope are true and details that we refuse to acknowledge, even to ourselves. God walked with me that day and I knew in my spirit that I shouldn't feel the way I did. I don't remember admitting that trouble lay ahead. For almost forty years I told myself that I never saw the fat, crazy-obvious Dot. Maybe I talked myself out of the knowledge provided by the Holy Spirit by convincing myself that I made too much of too little. Eventually, I settled on the explanation that my concerns were reasonable considering the two previous stressful weeks.

Looking backward, it's easy to see that God Dot of warning, guidance, and discernment—an obvious signal to change course, back out of the wedding, and head in another direction. But I didn't see it. The truth is, I knew that I was afraid, because the only people I knew in Omaha were his family and I didn't have a job yet. I wasn't even sure which direction was east. My family wasn't involved in the wedding, so it was just me and the in-laws. Fear won the day, and we were married. Five minutes after the "I do" part, I knew I'd made a huge mistake. But God, in His wisdom and stewardship, wastes nothing. Like every experience, this one helped make me who I am, and God uses it for His purpose every now and again to help another woman who married an unbalanced and dangerous man.

Faith is always a component of which God Dots you see and which you don't. A powerful example is found in 2 Kings 6, when Elisha and his people appear to be dramatically outnumbered by an enemy army. This is a God Dot the size of which few ever see.

> *Therefore he [the king of Syria] sent horses and chariots and a great army there, and they came by night and surrounded the city. And when the servant of the man of God arose early and went out, there was an army, surrounding the city with horses and chariots. And his servant said to him, "Alas, my master! What shall we do?"*
> *So he answered, "Do not fear, for those who are with us are more than those who are with them." And Elisha prayed, and said, "Lord, I pray, open his eyes that he may see." Then the Lord opened the eyes of the young man, and he saw. And behold, the mountain was full of horses and chariots of fire all around Elisha. So when the Syrians came down to him, Elisha prayed to the Lord, and said, "Strike this people, I pray, with blindness." And He struck them with blindness according to the word of Elisha.*
> *Now Elisha said to them, "This is not the way, nor is this the city. Follow me, and I will bring you to the man whom you seek." But he led them to Samaria.*

> *So it was, when they had come to Samaria, that Elisha said, "Lord, open the eyes of these men, that they may see." And the Lord opened their eyes, and they saw; and there they were, inside Samaria!*
> — 2 Kings 6:14-20

When the king of Israel asked Elisha if the captives should be killed, he said no, but rather to serve them a feast before sending them back to their master. The heart of Elisha's man was emboldened by his God Dot and the blindness of the enemy was enough to win the day. Kind treatment after capture may have also cooled any fire of retribution hidden in the captured soldiers' hearts because the Syrians never returned to Israel.

God Dots mark intimate moments when the Lord reaches out to reveal something only you recognize. They also illuminate places of momentous opportunity. Your Father is a personal God, not some faraway disconnected deity. He wants you to reflexively see what's powerful instead of what's broken, to see the beauty and potential of a situation instead of what is petty or some possible pitfall, to see light instead of darkness, and to see His truth everywhere. God wants you to feel His presence, see His influence, and build a faith that is powerful enough to move His kingdom on earth forward without a crutch.

As a friend and I were walking on the trail in the midst of Coronavirus lockdowns, she shared her concerns with current political, social, and cultural chaos. She was confident in Christ but still harbored fear of the unknown.

Even strong believers have moments of doubt or weakness, and I reminded her that the fight is not against flesh and blood, "but against principalities, against powers, against the rulers of the darkness of this age, against spiritual hosts of wickedness in the heavenly places" (Ephesians 6:12).

If you have concerns of your own about what's coming next or what the future holds for your children, please know that God is there and that nothing happens outside His awareness and will. Jesus was and is there for you the same way He is there for your children and grandchildren. Salvation is only available to individuals, not families, congregations, or nations.

> *This He set aside, nailing it to the cross. Having disarmed principalities and powers, He made a public spectacle of them, triumphing over them.* — Colossians 2:14-15

Almost everything we see is on the worldly plane, but I tell you with conviction that something huge is happening beyond your mortal vision. Imagine that you could see the armies of God stationed around you as Elisha did. Even if you saw tens of thousands or hundreds of thousands of enemy troops at the gate, God has a greater number poised and ready to strike. The war is already won and all it took to defeat Elisha's enemy was removing the ability to see. Guard your own vision by practicing the presence of God and expecting to see His markers.

One of the most common reasons people don't see more God Dots is because they don't look for them. I don't mean that they don't want to see them or don't wish to see them, but that their brains are trained to see other things more. When you walk outdoors, what do you see first, shadows or brilliant sunshine? Your brain processes what it thinks you need. To push some things to the front others are excluded.

There are two spirits in the world, the Spirit of God and the other one. What have you trained yourself to see, that which is holy or evil? Do you scan the horizon for goodness or worry so much about avoiding the darkness that you're constantly watching for it? What do you look for most, evidence of Christ in your life or evidence that the devil lurks nearby?

Are you an abundance person or a scarcity person? What you look at most creates a habit your brain honors. The good news is that whether you're two or ninety-two, your brain can change what it habitually sees.

In a 1999 study[1], cognitive psychologists Daniel Simons and Christopher Chabris proved that people can focus so hard on something that they become blind to the unexpected, even when staring right at it. If you develop "inattentional blindness," you miss details you don't expect to see. In the experiment, people were asked to watch a video[2] of two groups of people pass around basketballs—some dressed in white, some in black. The volunteers were asked to count the passes among players dressed in white while ignoring the passes of those in black. The degree of difficulty was high because the ball passers never stopped moving, weaving in and out of a circle like a human braid. Following white shirts and the balls was tough. The kicker is that half of the watchers missed the person in a gorilla suit walking in and out of the scene thumping its chest.

"Gorilla? There wasn't a gorilla." Except that there was.

THE GOD DOT

The researchers repeated the exercise ten years later with a twist. Everyone knew about the gorilla and watched for it, but they missed two other unexpected events. I tested myself by watching the new video[3]. Like everyone else who knew about the original study, I saw the gorilla and marveled that anyone missed it, but totally failed to see the other surprises because my brain was hooked on looking for the gorilla and watching the girls pass basketballs. Even after watching the video again, knowing there were two abnormalities, I only caught one.

Our brains see what they expect to see and fail to see the unexpected. Which explains why those who expect to see God present and active in their lives do so and those who don't, don't. I wasn't in the habit of seeing God Dots back in 1977 when I experienced the uneasiness prior to my wedding, but I remember the moment because of the marker God laid down that revealed itself years later.

Sometimes God Dots feel as if they've gone into hibernation like hedgehogs—unseen, unheard, and absent from daily life. I've experienced seasons of conversation with God so clear that I could dictate what I heard including inflection and punctuation. In other seasons, His voice was absent although I know that He was not. These quiet places can be periods of testing or times of distraction.

God Dots: *Similar to having spots before your eyes, only they're light bulbs that enlighten your brain, and you know God has spoken to you.*
— TJ Mulder

TWELVE
DISTRACTION DEMENTIA

If then you were raised with Christ, seek those things which are above, where Christ is, sitting at the right hand of God. Set your mind on things above, not on things on the earth.
Colossians 3:1-2

Sometimes God Dots hide in plain sight, rendered invisible because your brain is trained to see everything but God's presence in your life. Busyness is a frequent culprit, because it fractures your concentration and inhibits your ability to tick off goals met and progress made. Paul wrote Timothy that the love of money is the root of all evil, but in this twenty-first-century world, an avalanche of distractions purposefully sweeps God Dots under your mental carpet to let all that isn't God take center stage.

The Alzheimer's Association defines dementia as "a general term for loss of memory, language, problem-solving and other thinking abilities that are severe enough to interfere with daily life." Distraction dementia isn't a medical condition, but the irritating inability to recall details about everyday life or to access your full vocabulary because of the 17,413 things competing for your attention in any given moment.

Internet tracking systems use cookies (a horrible disservice to edible cookies) to stalk you by recording every touch, tap, or click. How often do you look at some product or service and then notice ads for it popping up everywhere? That's the dark side of power. On the lighter side, God also knows every thought, whim, touch, tap, and movement you make. I'll be thinking about or studying some topic when suddenly that subject comes up in conversation and I see the Dot.

There are many times I've read something or gained new understanding about part of my work or figured out a simpler way to explain something right before I get asked a question about it. Seeing God Dots never gets old and God's timing is perfect. These are moments of preparation and provision I didn't know about in advance. The Lord never asks us to do something without providing the means or ability. Whether the internet or the universe, everything is connected, and you're being stalked both electronically and spiritually.

> *For the eyes of the Lord run to and fro throughout the whole earth, to show Himself strong on behalf of those whose heart is loyal to Him.* —2 Chronicles 16:9

THE GOD DOT

> *Discipline yourselves, keep alert. Like a roaring lion your adversary the devil prowls around, looking for someone to devour. Resist him, steadfast in your faith, for you know that your brothers and sisters in all the world are undergoing the same kinds of suffering.* —1 Peter 5:8-9

Everything God does, Satan tries to imitate.

This may be a rude revelation for someone, but what you see online is what you look at most. You're being trained to look anywhere but toward God and not to think for even ten seconds at a time, which makes it impossible to hear the Holy Spirit. Ten seconds of quiet and peace isn't enough to prepare you to be receptive to the still small voice of the Spirit. When's the last time you sat down to pray and realized minutes later that you quit praying a long time ago?

We don't see God Dots because our memory cards are full. Back in the sixties it was fun to see how many people you could cram into a VW Beetle. The first few into the Bug could see parts of the interior, but by the time the last knee and elbow were inside, and the doors closed, they could only see the few inches directly in front of their eyes. Folks were stuck.

The Reticular Activating System (RAS) is a coordinated mass of nerves in your brainstem that lets important information in by filtering out what it considers unnecessary. Within months after buying my 2008 burnt orange Jeep Patriot I started seeing Patriots everywhere. When I began riding motorcycles in 1979, I noticed every bike on the street. Show me a pack of fifty dogs and I'll know if there's a dachshund present in a split second.

The RAS is the reason you hear your name in a crowded room when nothing else rises above the din. The RAS sifts out white noise, and only the information or messages that make it through the filter get converted into conscious thoughts, emotions, or both. Anything you are aware of survived the RAS screening process. What gets through is what's most important to you at the time.

> "Your RAS takes what you focus on and creates a filter for it. It then sifts through the data and presents only the pieces that are important to you. All of this happens without you noticing, of course. The RAS programs itself to work in your favor without you actively doing anything. Pretty awesome, right?
>
> In the same way, the RAS seeks information that validates your beliefs. It filters the world through the parameters you give it, and your beliefs shape those parameters. If you think you are bad at giving speeches, you probably will be. If you believe you work efficiently, you most likely do. The RAS helps you see what you want to see and in doing so, influences your actions." —Tobias van Schneider[1]

No matter your age, you can train your brain to look for God Dots by telling your RAS that they're important to you and you want to see them. Program the fact of His presence into your mind through Bible study, talking with others daily about the ways He appears in your life, and by documenting your own Dot appearances. Make God Dots a daily habit and you'll begin seeing them everywhere.

My usual breakfast is a boiled egg and buttered toast at my desk. I make a half-dozen boiled eggs at one time, so I'm set for six days without having to think about anything more than popping bread into the toaster oven. No muss, no fuss, no decisions, and no clean up. One day I opened the fridge to pull out an egg but couldn't find the plastic container. I asked my husband, "Did you finish the boiled eggs?"

"Nope. But I saw them in the freezer earlier."

"What are they doing in the freezer?"

"I don't know, you put them there."

The two remaining boiled eggs were frozen solid. In case you're wondering, frozen boiled eggs don't thaw well. Why did I stash the egg container in the freezer? Dunno, but stuff like that happens. Like putting the half-full Mr. Coffee carafe in the cupboard or finding myself in the bedroom with no clue about why I'm there. Some days I wonder if a prankster Mr. Hyde alter ego likes to mess with my Dr. Jekyll. Be honest, have you ever looked for your phone while you were talking on it? Or couldn't find your glasses because you were wearing them?

You can blame distraction dementia for most of these exasperating moments. Most folks I know suffer from it to some degree. The greatest cause of distraction dementia is brain overload. According to Eric Schmidt, former Google CEO, the same amount of information created from the dawn of human history until 2003 is now created daily. Author

Douglas Rushkoff coined the term *Digiphrenia*, to describe an emerging global health threat, which is the abnormal state of mental activity resulting from the constant bombardment of digital input.

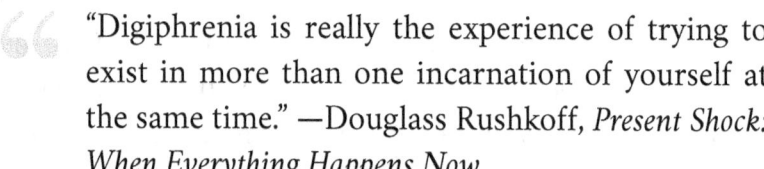

> "Digiphrenia is really the experience of trying to exist in more than one incarnation of yourself at the same time." —Douglass Rushkoff, *Present Shock: When Everything Happens Now*

PEOPLE ROUTINELY LIVE in multiple environments at once. While sitting at a cozy table in your favorite pizza place with your spouse, you fight off the urge to check Facebook so you don't miss something important that one of your friends is doing. You're not trying to ignore your spouse, but because you're busy posting images of your bubbling hot pepperoni pie to Instagram— plus trying to follow a text thread with your mother in Sausalito, your attention wandered.

"I'm sorry, sweetie, what were you saying?"

Did you ever look for something in the refrigerator you know is there but can't find it? When this happens to me, I ask my husband to please look on my behalf. He opens the door and there it is, front and center, laughing at me. That happens because my mind is occupied on another channel and I literally cannot see what is staring me in the face.

At other times we look for something we remember as being about a foot tall and four inches wide. Doors are thrown open, cabinets are searched, closets rummaged through, and storage boxes inspected. But it's nowhere to be found. On a final assault, we decide to empty the first cabinet we looked in. Before it's bare, we find the item right where we thought it would be. The problem is that it isn't a foot tall and four inches wide, it's nine inches tall and six inches wide. Our brains didn't see it because it didn't fit our preset parameters.

And we wonder why we don't see God in the world more often.

> *Now it happened as they went that He entered a certain village; and a certain woman named Martha welcomed Him into her house. And she had a sister called Mary, who also sat at Jesus' feet and heard His Word. But Martha was distracted with much serving, and she approached Him and said, "Lord, do You not care that my sister has left me to serve alone? Therefore tell her to help me."*
> *And Jesus answered and said to her, "Martha, Martha, you are worried and troubled about many things. But one thing is needed, and Mary has chosen that good part, which will not be taken away from her."*
> —Luke 10:38-42

Decision Fatigue

> "The word "decide" shares an etymological root with "homicide," the Latin word "caedere," meaning "to cut down" or "to kill," and that loss looms especially large when decision fatigue sets in." —New York Times Magazine[2]

Making strings of decisions exhausts your brain in much the same way continuous physical exertion tires your body. When you reach the end of your mental energy reserves, you look for the easy way out, settling on whatever's simplest or nearest because you can't make one more thoughtful decision. It's shocking the number of little decisions we make every day, especially early in the day, leaving the afternoon and evening vulnerable to "whatever I have to do to get it over with."

The ability to think creativity and be productive erodes with every decision you make.

"White toast or wheat toast?"

"How crisp do I want it today?"

"Green plate or white plate?"

"Peanut butter, Nutella, or margarine?"

"Use the knife lying next to the sink to spread my butter or get a clean one out of the drawer?"

"Wait for the toaster to pop or look to see who just texted me?"

"Okay, I got that text taken care of, should I look to see if there are others?"

"Gracious, I have fifty-three unopened emails. I wonder if there's anything important."

[Forty-three minutes later...]

"Did I make toast this morning?"

. . .

THE GOD DOT

You haven't made it past breakfast and you've already burned somewhere between one hundred and ten thousand small decisions from whether to get out of bed now or wait a few minutes to whether to put on jeans or sweatpants, and no matter which you choose you still must decide which pair to stick your legs into. Add a spouse, kids, pets, and weather to the equation, not to mention every electronic device you know better than your mother, and you're on the fast track to mental exhaustion. Texts and emails require a decision to read now or wait until later. Everyone has a unique point at which decision fatigue sets in. There's a reason creative people tend to work first thing in the morning while their brains are still fresh and firing on all cylinders. It's the same reason Steve Jobs always wore a black turtleneck and jeans. Routine fashion decisions are seldom the best use of scarce energy reserves.

My habit was getting the have-to chores done in the morning and then spending time with the Lord. But He expects the first fruits of our day because that's the time when our spirit, mind, and body are most rested and powerful. So now I get up, throw on walking clothes I left out the night before, feed the dog, and then head out to the walking trail with woods, forest creatures, and God. There's nothing between us but sky. Those moments are the richest and most creative of my day and when I feel most connected to everything invisible to my aging blue eyes.

It's curious how many God Dots happen early in the day. Maybe that's because we're more likely to recognize them before decision fatigue reduces us to feeling that being an adult is exhausting and we're done making choices. When my husband asks what we're having for dinner he isn't suggesting that I actually make food. The day we met I told him that I don't cook. He asks because he suffers from the same decision fatigue I do. We honestly don't care what we eat because it's another decision piling on at the end of the day and our decision bridge is burned until tomorrow.

Switch Tasking

> "When we think we're multitasking we're actually multiswitching. That is what the brain is very good at doing—quickly diverting its attention from one place to the next. We think we're being productive. We are, indeed, being busy. But in reality we're simply giving ourselves extra work." —Michael Harris, *The End of Absence: Reclaiming What We've Lost in a World of Constant Connection*

Some folks believe that multitasking is a natural ability or learned skill, allowing them to juggle a few or many different things at once. I used to be one of those people. The truth first dawned on me more than fifteen years ago when I was making a scratch pie crust while talking to my best friend on the telephone. Cooking and baking aren't the same, and for years I made main-course mincemeat pies for Christmas dinner.

I don't remember how I screwed up, but I had to pitch the crust and start over after hanging up. Even back then, I told her that I'd lost a step when it came to multitasking. Since then, I've learned that no one truly multitasks. I may suffer from distraction dementia, but parts of my memory are fine. Even though I haven't been in that ranch kitchen for fifteen years, I can still see the black Ubatuba granite countertop with green and gold flecks showcasing a miserable lump of bad dough.

Does driving a car while talking on the phone count as multitasking? In 2020, forty-eight states, the District of Columbia, Puerto Rico, Guam, and the U.S. Virgin Islands banned texting while driving because folks really aren't that good at multitasking.

Distractions prevent you from targeted focus, often leaching your attention away from what's most important. If the greatest temptation you face is distraction from the goal you hope to achieve or closing the gap between the vision God gave you and making it to the finish line, you need to take a serious look at decluttering your life. Each time your focus pulls away from the presence of God it's a win for the other side.

Your ability to remember, see God Dots, or make wise choices is diminished because so much of your available mental space and decision energy is used for unimportant stuff. It's similar to a hoarder who puts her sacked garbage in the bedroom closet. Soon there's no room for clothes, and all she sees is garbage. What clothes were in the closet to begin with are hidden by worthless trash. Storage unit facilities multiply faster than rabbits because so many houses that were huge when the family moved in are now too small to hold their stuff. Possessions go wherever there's room, not in places that make sense.

"I know I have that somewhere…"

Somewhere is useless unless you know where somewhere is. It's like forgetting the name of your eldest first cousin or your middle grandchild's birthday. You know it's in there somewhere, but you can't find it.

Using your brain energy wisely is a function of stewardship.

Teach your RAS filter what to show you.

Be a Mary, not a Martha, and reserve your attention for Jesus Christ. Let dinner wait.

If you develop the habit of looking for God Dots, you'll see them everywhere. If you look at other stuff, you'll miss the Dots and you'll miss God.

> "Knowledge isn't power. The right use of knowledge is power. (It's called wisdom.) We like to consume food when we're bored, confused, overwhelmed, or uninspired. Guess what? We do the same thing with content. When we get bored, confused, overwhelmed, and uninspired, we often distract ourselves by consuming more content. The problem is that most people don't even apply ten percent of what they already know. More content offers the illusion of progress and accomplishment. They rationalize that they are doing something: they're eating. But simply shoveling in more content only leaves them feeling guilty, fat, lazy, and undisciplined. Consuming empty calories hacks us. It's distracting, and it sucks up our limited energy and attention." —Kary Oberbrunner, the *Elixir Project Experience*

God Dot: *A divine awareness.* — Carousel

THIRTEEN

WHY DOTS MATTER

Finally, brethren, whatever things are true, whatever things are noble, whatever things are just, whatever things are pure, whatever things are lovely, whatever things are of good report, if there is any virtue and if there is anything praiseworthy—meditate on these things. The things which you learned and received and heard and saw in me, these do, and the God of peace will be with you.
Philippians 4:8-9

Happiness is making progress toward a good goal. God Dots are evidence of progress made as well as God's continuous presence and participation in your daily life. God Dot maps with only a few markers make it difficult to know where you're going much less if you're making progress. The more Dots you recognize and document, the greater your clarity of direction and confidence that you're moving forward. Therefore, the greater level of happiness and purpose you experience.

Progressive faith is one way to describe sanctification, the process of daily movement toward eternity, holiness, and immortality living in the presence of Jesus Christ and God Himself. There is no more profound God Dot that an encounter with Jesus. The road to Damascus transformed a rabid predator of Christians into the apostle who wrote most of the New Testament. Once called and tutored by Jesus, Paul was personally transformed and played a significant role in the life of every Christian since the mid-first century AD.

The major God Dots of Jesus's journey are recorded in the Bible between Genesis 1 and Revelation 22. The Cross is the center of time and experience, the climax of human history and its future. The focus of Calvary is three crosses—the central sagging form of a wounded and dying Christ with crucified criminals on either side. Whether the two men were thieves, robbers, or guilty of other crimes, all we know for certain is what God's Word reveals. There's no information about their lives except that they ended on Calvary. The most important takeaway is that these two men died a shameful death, but because they encountered Christ, they experienced two distinctly different eternal outcomes.

At the first, even the thieves, already crucified and soon to die themselves, mocked Jesus.

> *There were also two others, criminals, led with Him to be put to death. And when they had come to the place called Calvary, there they crucified Him, and*

> *the criminals, one on the right hand and the other on the left. Then Jesus said, "Father, forgive them, for they do not know what they do."*
> *And they divided His garments and cast lots. And the people stood looking on. But even the rulers with them sneered, saying, "He saved others; let Him save Himself if He is the Christ, the chosen of God." The soldiers also mocked Him, offering Him sour wine, and saying, "If You are the King of the Jews, save Yourself." And an inscription also was written over Him in letters of Greek, Latin, and Hebrew:*
> THIS IS THE KING OF THE JEWS.
> *Then one of the criminals who were hanged blasphemed Him, saying, "If You are the Christ, save Yourself and us." But the other, answering, rebuked him, saying, "Do you not even fear God, seeing you are under the same condemnation? And we indeed justly, for we receive the due reward of our deeds; but this Man has done nothing wrong." Then he said to Jesus, "Lord, remember me when You come into Your kingdom." And Jesus said to him, "Assuredly, I say to you, today you will be with Me in Paradise."*
> — Luke 23:32-43

One thief, clinging to his derisive pride, ridiculed the Lamb of God while the other experienced transformation. As remains the case today, salvation follows repentance. The penitent thief acknowledged Jesus as Lord, asked for mercy, and received it. There are two distinct eternal outcomes; one with Jesus and one without. Encountering Christ is the fork in the road.

Which thief you meet and which eternity you experience depends on what happens when you meet Jesus.

God Dots matter.

God brought the kingdom of heaven to earth through His Son, our Lord and Savior Jesus Christ. In this church age, the end time of human history, that model remains in effect. The kingdom of God is visible in the world through God Dots and through obedient and blessed Christ-followers. You were created for a unique and specific purpose. Your journey began before God established linear time and continues into eternity. Mortal life is your collective experience in relationship to the creation, to the created, and to the Dot Creator.

There are no coincidences and no chance encounters. Any time you wrestle with conscience or fear, hearing yourself whine, "Why me?"—the moment is significant. More than likely, you're standing dead center on a pivotal God Dot. In the Book of Esther, the young queen faces a choice between personal security and risking her life to save her people by seeking the opportunity to address her husband the king. Under Persian law, no one could approach the king with impunity, not even the missus. Esther's uncle Mordecai puts her choice in these simple terms:

> *For if you remain completely silent at this time, relief and deliverance will arise for the Jews from another place, but you and your father's house will perish. Yet who knows whether you have come to the kingdom for such a time as this?* —Esther 4:14

The silent voice you hear arguing that the choice before you today isn't all that important is true in one sense but a heinous lie in another. Whatever your decision to move forward, even if made in uncertainty or fear, won't ultimately affect God's bigger plan, but it may affect your future. Your circumstance isn't the product of chance nor is the obstacle you face random. The only way to know if this is your *such a time* is to look back later and see what God did with it. I believe we have many *such a times* in life. The language used in the Book of Esther suggests that the queen's *for such a time* was both present and continuing.

Royal titles and finery offered Queen Esther no more protection than church membership, memorizing Scripture, contributing to missions, or endless service offer you. The critical points in Esther's story are awareness, obedience, and commitment regardless of the cost. In the preceding verse (4:13), Mordecai's message to Queen Esther is clear, "Do not think in your heart that you will escape in the king's palace any more than all the other Jews."

Esther's story is profound in both warning, promise, and blessing. Even as queen, the odds of approaching the throne without an invitation were slim. Unless summoned, no one could bother the king and only the foolish dared push the envelope. Sometimes obedience brings mortal destruction, but like Stephen in Acts 7, God uses the example for those who follow later. The Bible is replete with patterns and types. Consider what we know of Stephen's martyrdom: he was falsely accused, his face appeared as an angel to his detractors, he was obedient unto death, he asked God to receive his spirit, and then he petitioned His Lord to forgive those who killed him.

Think back to Calvary and notice how Stephen followed Jesus's example in the moments before he died. Unlike Esther, you enjoy the freedom to approach the throne of God whenever you wish because the blood of Jesus cleanses the stain of sin from the saved. Not only is God accessible without fear of penalty, but being in His presence, whether in spirit or by recognizing a God Dot, you receive blessing, assurance, and an infusion of spiritual light.

God Dot: *God's active presence in my life.* — Jane E. Harber

FOURTEEN
DOT ERASERS

But even if our gospel is veiled, it is veiled to those who are perishing, whose minds the god of this age has blinded, who do not believe, lest the light of the gospel of the glory of Christ, who is the image of God, should shine on them.
2 Corinthians 4:3-4

The Lord expects you to share your successes, failures, lessons, and spiritual insight with others. Like any physical body, the body of Christ must communicate among its various parts to function well. This is why I'm sharing moments of amazement with you, times when I felt lifted beyond the usual boundaries of human experience by God's presence as well as instances where I missed the mark or worse, I forgot a specific message.

God Dots can be seen, processed, and then disappear for a time, or even for the rest of your mortal days. Documenting your Dots is imperative but isn't an iron-clad guarantee that you'll be able to access the record later.

Dots are erased in a number of ways.

These are four that I've experienced:

1. Forgetfulness

2. Failing to record them

3. God removes them from memory

4. Satan's scheme

1. Forgetfulness

> "Forgetting doesn't take special effort. It just happens, it's our gravitational pull. If we don't attend to God's words and works, we lose our delight in them. We lose our way, we lose perspective. God's people's biggest danger is forgetting their story—who they are and whose they are." —David Horner

You already know about two times I forgot a big God Dot. It still annoys me when I think about it, but there it is. The first was when I was asked to write *Rapture and Revelation*, ran into doubt and difficulty, quit, and then forgot the assignment—twice. The second was when God told me that He would send a forever home for Journey. Time passed, but instead of it being pushed to the back by an obstacle, I forgot because I enjoyed the path I shared with Journey too much to remember. At least that's the best way I have to understand what happened. Both seem ridiculous in hindsight yet prove that memory has its own mind and habit that you must know and resist.

The task and responsibility to record and remember is a biblical constant. Consider the following scriptures. God knows that memory isn't reliable and commands us to take action.

> *For what great nation is there that has God so near to it, as the Lord our God is to us, for whatever reason we may call upon Him? Only take heed to yourself, and diligently keep yourself, lest you forget the things your eyes have seen, and lest they depart from your heart all the days of your life. And teach them to your children and your grandchildren.*
> — Deuteronomy 4:7, 9

> *Then it shall be, if you by any means forget the Lord your God, and follow other gods, and serve them and worship them, I testify against you this day that you shall surely perish.*
> — Deuteronomy 8:19

> *I will meditate on Your precepts,*
> *And contemplate Your ways.*
> *I will delight myself in Your statutes;*
> *I will not forget Your word.* —Psalm 119:15-16

> *For this they willfully forget: that by the Word of God the heavens were of old, and the earth standing out of water and in the water, by which the world that then existed perished, being flooded with water. But the heavens and the earth which are now preserved by the same word, are reserved for fire until the day of judgment and perdition of ungodly men. But, beloved, do not forget this one thing, that with the Lord one day is as a thousand years, and a thousand years as one day.* —2 Peter 3:5-8

To forget our story is to forget who we are and why we're here. No wonder *remembering* is such a central theme in Scripture. God knows the gravitational pull of human awareness, which draws us inexorably toward forgetfulness. God's people are always in danger of losing both their individual and collective memory, forgetting who they are and whose they are.

2. Failing to Record Them

The fastest way to erase a God Dot is to live a normal life. The imperative to document your Dot experiences is a major theme of this book. Whenever you need a refresher, review the chapters "Distraction Dementia" and "Collecting Your Dots."

3. God Removes the Memory

> "Let me remind you that this is God's universe, and He is doing things His way. You may think you have a better way, but you don't have a universe to rule." —J. Vernon McGee

One of my most interesting memories is remarkable because I don't remember much about it. I know that sounds odd, but walking with the Lord is more of an adventure than a process or system. One morning years ago, I suddenly understood everything there was to understand about relationship between a mortal and the Creator of the universe and ran to my computer, pouring five thousand words of pure revelation into a WORD document. The next day I went to open the file because I couldn't remember a single word, but it wasn't there. It was if it never existed. The drive was expertly searched but the file was gone without a trace. Details of the revelation are deeply buried in a place I can't access today, but the sense of peace, confidence, and expectation I felt burns as brightly now as it did then.

The Bible shares stories about Spirit-led forgetfulness or unawareness. Consider these and remember, God's ways are not our ways.

> *I know a man in Christ who fourteen years ago—whether in the body I do not know, or whether out of the body I do not know, God knows—such a one was caught up to the third heaven. And I know such a man—whether in the body or out of the body I do not know, God knows— how he was caught up into Paradise and heard inexpressible words, which it is not lawful for a man to utter.* —2 Corinthians 12:2-4

> *"But you, Daniel, shut up the words and seal the book, until the time of the end. Many shall run to and fro,*

and knowledge shall increase." He said, "Go your way, Daniel, for the words are shut up and sealed until the time of the end." —Daniel 12:4, 9

SOMEWHERE BACK IN the 1990s I watched a television documentary about a central American woman with stigmata, the periodic appearance of wounds, scars, and pain in the hands, wrists, and feet, corresponding with the crucifixion wounds of Jesus Christ. Saint Francis of Assisi rejoiced in such suffering late in his life. In the documentary, the late middle-aged woman lay still and calm on a bed of pain. I can still see her face because of what happened next. The camera zoomed in on her eyes, and I saw a reflection. It was the face of Jesus. I knew it without a doubt before the camera zoomed back out. Peace, power, assurance, and joy flooded my spirit, and I wrote everything down on the inside cover of a special book I kept in an old oak secretary desk in my closet. The book disappeared. For years I thought that I was inexcusably careless to lose track of something so precious. Now I know that while the record wasn't mine to keep, the knowing is.

God does whatever it takes to get you on the Dot Line designed for you, even if it means removing a message that delivered a faith explosion.

4. Satan's Scheme

> "God has ordained that Satan have a long leash with God holding on to the leash because he knows that when we walk in and out of those

temptations, struggling with both the physical effects that they bring and the moral effects that they bring, more of God's glory will shine." —John Piper

One phrase in the Lord's Prayer that inspires question is, "Lead us not into temptation, but deliver us from the evil one." God doesn't tempt you, but He permits Satan to do so. Once Jesus was baptized and the Spirit of God lit on Him as a dove, the scene quickly changes to a wilderness of temptation. The Spirit led Him there, but Satan is the only tempter. None of us can defend ourselves the way Christ did, but we have the same Spirit to support our efforts. The more I study distraction the more I believe it to be one of the most powerful temptations used by the devil to steal your focus from God.

When I pray this phrase, I expand it to include awareness, asking for the ability to recognize whatever temptations try to limit the time I spend in the presence of God. Too many small God Dots, intimate markers of His presence in your daily life, are lost to the noise, bumps, alarms, and pressures of the world because you forgot them before you had the chance to write them down.

Distraction dementia is real. The devil cackles with glee with every God Dot lost to memory. Satan is the Dot Eraser. Recognize this opportunistic foe and learn to defend your Dots from his twisted fingers. If you have any doubts that he's a real actor in your life, consider the following scriptures.

> *Now there was a day when the sons of God came to present themselves before the Lord, and Satan also*

came among them. The Lord said to Satan, "From where have you come?" Satan answered the Lord and said, "From going to and fro on the earth, and from walking up and down on it."—Job 1:6-7

For we do not wrestle against flesh and blood, but against principalities, against powers, against the rulers of the darkness of this age, against spiritual hosts of wickedness in the heavenly places. — Ephesians 6:12

We know that we are from God, and the whole world lies in the power of the evil one.—1 John 5:19

I HAD A WEIRD DREAM, in which I felt that God set into motion events leading to a series of major life changes, like who I was married to. In the dream I was fine with that and everyone else seemed to be fine with it as well, at least on the surface. Aside from failing basic logic tests, dreams don't necessarily reveal what other characters are thinking. While I wasn't eager to make the change, I am reflexively obedient, delighting in the will of the Father once I understand it. The whole dream was matter of fact, but as we got closer to implementing the changes, I began to harbor a few tiny doubts. I told myself that since this came from the Lord, going through with it was obedience, right?

While still in the dream, I remembered a lesson the Holy Spirit taught me about the Word of God on a related topic nearly thirty years earlier. The message was clear, that *everything is now by the book because you have both knowledge and understanding. We've talked about this before.* Which is the clear message of Hebrews 10:26 and raises an important point.

God never sends, arranges, or directs any thought, process, or event that disagrees with His Word. Changing spouses in a dream, no matter how much I thought the direction came from God, is in direct opposition to His Word. I knew then that the original plan did not come from God. It felt like it did, but it failed the only sure test. Don't be fooled when the Enemy tries to tell you that a God Dot isn't real. The sin in Genesis chapter three was believing the common-sense serpent over the Creator. Don't let the rabid Dot Eraser anywhere near your Dot map.

God Dots provide moments of clarity, especially when they reinforce the truth of His Word. He hasn't changed his mind or made one revision. God doesn't evolve.

There are only two spiritual commanders, the Lord God and Satan. Knowing the Dot Creator intimately and walking confidently in His vision for you is the only real defense against the Dot Eraser. Look for God Dots every day, meditate on them, record them, and remember to remember.

God Dots: *Unexpected God moments.* — Melinda LePage

FIFTEEN
YOUR UNIQUE DOTS

The LORD has called Me from the womb;
from the matrix of my mother He has made mention of My name.
Isaiah 49:1

Your God Dot journey is uniquely yours. No one else has your personality, spirit, or God-given purpose. You were created for the life you're living and to make it a testimony to the grace and power of the Lord. The Potter didn't make a mold for men when He formed Adam from the dust of the earth. The products of His workmanship aren't endless replicas of one original creation, each with a unique flaw from the firing process. Every new creation has the same profound flaw, made fixable through the Lord Jesus Christ. But beyond that single blemish, we are each one-offs, and the Master Creator doesn't make spare parts.

God has an exclusive vision for each person. Some kingdom leaders serve as parents, raising godly children, preparing a new generation to carry God's vision for them across the finish line. Whatever platform God asks you to build, the size isn't material to its importance to the body of Christ because there is no hierarchy of importance among His people. I've yet to meet anyone remotely like Elijah, Moses, or Joseph, but I've met many fine saints who effectively walk out their calling in ways the world considers unremarkable. Who has a greater effect on the future of faith than husbands and wives who become fathers and mothers, faithfully modeling the character and teachings of Jesus Christ to their children and communities?

> *Train up a child in the way he should go, and when he is old he will not depart from it.*
> —Proverbs 22:6

New Creations in Christ are defined by the indwelling Holy Spirit (John 3:5-7). That means that the kingdom of God is within you (Luke 17:20-21), and so is the Holy Spirit. You can't see your personality, but it's there and you act upon it constantly. Certain things, sounds, or aromas leap out at you because you have a natural affinity or preference for them.

When my father was in his last months of life, I spent a lot of time with him and my stepmother. The three-hour drive seemed shorter every time I made it because the landmarks along the road grew familiar and predictable—until the day I saw a turquoise CJ7 Jeep parked in an unmarked lot halfway between our home and theirs. I felt an immediate connection to it as well as a passion to own it. I didn't stop that day, but my mind kept playing imaginary movies of me sitting in the driver's seat of that adorable vehicle, feeling the metal bucket beneath the unpadded seat, smoothly moving through the gearbox, and styling around town or breezing down the highway. The Jeep kept reminding me that it was out there waiting and that we belonged together.

The next week I stopped to snap a photo and touch the Jeep. We even enjoyed a lilting conversation although it never spoke a word. I shot a video as I walked around it to show my dad and my husband because I decided to find out who owned it and if they'd put a price on it. I didn't notice the names but remembered that there was a feed store and automotive repair shop across the road from the farm lot where the Jeep was parked. An internet search for repair shops in the area produced a likely candidate so I called to see if anyone knew who owned the Jeep.

"Oh sure, it belongs to Ron. He's at the feed store."

I got the phone number and called Ron. He was a hobby auto trader and had owned the Jeep for several years. He was also honest. It ran, he told me, but probably needed a new battery and had a lot of rust on the undercarriage. I jotted down the details, asked the price, and told him I'd call him the next Saturday if I wanted to look at it. When Dad watched the video, he told me to buy it. But then, Dad loved the pursuit of toys with engines, so I didn't let his opinion bring too much weight to my decision. My husband wasn't against it, so I researched what it would take to bring the turquoise CJ7 back to finely tuned operation.

When I set out for Dad's house the next week, I intended to buy the Jeep. When I was less than a mile from where it waited for me, I still hadn't called Ron. I drove by without stopping, thinking that I could always do it on the way home. The practical side of my personality slapped the creative side back to reality. Not only was it a ridiculously impractical vehicle, but it had a stick shift, and my bad knees can't manage a clutch anymore. Besides, where would I store it? It didn't even have air conditioning.

I didn't buy it because I knew that the season of life the Jeep called to was over. That rust-enhanced turquoise beauty was so me, but a me from decades earlier. Even so, I was relieved when it was no longer in the parking lot along the road. But it sure was a powerfully cute turquoise CJ7.

You know which truck you like best, which dog breed speaks to you, which delicacy in the bakery case has your name on it, or which pair of shoes you just have to own. You can't see your personality, but it's there all the time, and your home, closet, and garage reflect it into the world. When you say that something has your name written all over it, you mean that it's just your style and meant for you. If a car, puppy, or cookie identifies itself so clearly, then God Dots should be at least as obvious as that last piece of triple fudge chocolate cake that spoke so eloquently to you last Sunday.

IN MID-SEPTEMBER, the coolness of early autumn in north Texas and the verdant aftermath of two huge rains were unexpected blessings. I took notice, offered praise, and delighted in the shade produced by still-lush trees, enthusiastic bird song, and precious time alone with God under a limitless heaven.

The Holy Spirit is a superpower available to every New Creation in Christ. Walking along, I concentrated on being present, tuning my spiritual receiver to hear from the Lord—to recognize and tap into that power. Then the thought popped into my mind that I hadn't seen a deer for several weeks. I kept walking, but said aloud, "Lord, I would love to see a deer."

Since I asked, I scanned the woods on my left. There, in perfect profile, backlit by filtered sunlight, a magnificent buck stood grazing. He lifted his head and looked directly at me, and I told him that he was gorgeous. If I'd continued walking, eyes looking straight ahead, I would have missed the gift—the God Dot—the Yes. Gift received! I thanked the Lord and walked on. The Holy Spirit heard me say I'd like to see a deer and less than five seconds later there he was. Delighted with this God Dot, I began thinking about the difference between God delivering and withholding.

A moment later, I happened to look to my right—and saw two more deer just a few feet off the trail, a doe and her fawn, the fawn big enough that his tail was as striking as his mother's and his spots completely gone. Looking to my right at that precise moment wasn't a coincidence. I had time to introduce myself to mother and son and asked for God to assure them that I presented no danger. The three of us chatted a bit, the fawn flagging his huge white tail up and down, and then they moved peacefully into the woods.

You can't see the side of your nose, but you know it's there. It's possible to see God Dots all the time because He's there with you and never takes a coffee break. If I didn't glance off the trail when I did, would the deer have been there? If so, they would have been God Dots missed.

Some folks say, "I'm a believer, but not all that spiritual," which is curious. How can anyone indwelled by God's Spirit not be spiritual? The same Holy Spirit lives in each child of the King although sanctification is the work of a lifetime. The work of bringing you into right relationship with the Father is finished. It was finished on the Cross.

Thinking that you're not enough of a saint to see God everywhere denies His transformative power. You may not see God Dots around you every day but there's nothing you need that you don't already have. You simply learn to look. Ask. Document. Get to know the Father more through His Word and in quiet time spent together in the expanse of His creation where no manmade barrier stands between you and Him. If your old man is dead and your new man lives in Christ, the powerful ability to walk in His presence today is not only possible but should call to you like Juliet to Romeo.

God has a special purpose and vision for you *for such a time as this*. There's no more wonderful place than being in the center of God's will. Seek it. Find it. Cherish it. Experience life on a level few people enjoy by refusing to believe that the power of Christ is limited by your limitations. Your spirit tells you that there is more. Listen.

"When we are who we are called to be, we will set the world ablaze." —St. Catherine of Sienna

When something happens you can't explain and wasn't expected, but is totally a blessing, that's a God Dot. — Susan Self (Kimmel)

SIXTEEN
A LINE OF DOTS

You, Lord, keep my lamp burning; my God turns my darkness into light.
Psalm 18:28

My father challenged me, pressured me, disapproved of me, disowned me, shamed me, and rejected me. But once I set immovable boundaries in my thirties, we eventually established a bond of friendship and mutual respect. There was much to appreciate about my father, but he was mercurial, switching from jovial to ugly, from light to dark in the space of a breath and for reasons only he understood. My dad was an amazing man, but like many others, was imperfect, harboring hidden insecurities, and hoping that his walk before the Lord was good enough to get him into heaven.

May 18, 2016

My father's breathing comes in moist heaving waves, the guttural sounds that often precede death becoming eerily familiar. Sitting in a kitchen chair positioned by the side of the rented hospital bed, I watch his face, so familiar, yet without the power and context of personality. I know this is the last time we'll be together this side of eternity because he is transitioning from mortality to immortality. My stepmother is asleep in her recliner on the other side of the small living room, confident that I'll wake her if there's reason. At eighty-eight years old, she is exhausted from the stress of caring for her non-ambulatory husband and the change she knows is coming.

This time with my father is a special gift from God, a privilege and celebration of a father-daughter relationship that didn't exist until the past few years. I love the man lying in the hospital bed in the corner of his living room. Only the grace of God makes this moment possible for me. My father knows that I love him, and I know that he loves me.

In the quiet of the first hours past midnight, I heard the familiar voice of the Lord say to me, "You have five years to get ready."

It wasn't audible, but it was distinct and clear.

"Five years to get ready for what?"

Silence.

Within the hour my father was gone. Or more precisely, he was now more fully alive than he'd ever been. I woke my stepmother and we confirmed that Dad was gone. We hugged one another tightly, praised God for this peaceful end, and I called the hospice nurse.

MAY 28, 2016, the night before my father's memorial service was routine. My husband and I planned to leave early to make the three-hour drive because we still had livestock and we'd just been to a granddaughter's high school graduation out of state and were scheduled to fly out the next morning for another granddaughter's wedding.

We didn't make the memorial or the wedding.

Not long after going to bed, my husband began feeling unwell, becoming violently nauseous and uncomfortable. Within two hours we knew that something was desperately wrong. He didn't want an ambulance, so I helped him to the car about 3:00 a.m. and drove to the Emergency Room. The desk clerk knew that he was in trouble and repeatedly called to the back to see if someone could get my husband into a bed. We waited. As minutes ticked by, he slumped lower in the wheelchair I used to get him in the door.

The large ER wasn't busy, and the clerk told us there was only one patient in the back. For some reason, until that person was transferred, they wouldn't let anyone else in for treatment.

Without even a guesstimate of when they could see my husband, I hauled him back to the car and drove to a nearby stand-alone Emergency Room. After stabilizing him, the ER docs transferred him back to the hospital we'd left a few hours earlier as a direct admission. No one refuses an ambulance.

A week later, I sat by my husband's bedside, fuzzy gray hospital-issue booties keeping my toes warm, my feet resting on the window side of the foot of his bed. He was critically ill. The only thing he'd said to me that day was to please stay, but not to talk. Listening took too much of his waning strength.

In the quiet of the moment, I heard a familiar voice say, "You have five years to get ready." Not audibly, but nevertheless, distinct and clear.

"Five years to get ready for what?"

Silence.

While my husband was still hospitalized, I had an early morning conversation with the Lord as I tried to grab a couple of hours sleep before morning chores and going back to the hospital. I fully understood that my husband and I might have reached the end of our "Till death do us part" time together. In the quiet darkness of our bedroom, I thought about living life alone. Who would I talk to besides myself? What happens to a partnership when one of the partners passes away? Who would I be without him? How would I handle the chores? What would I do during long evening hours alone? What happens to friendships when a couple becomes a single? I was sad, but strangely at peace. I said, "You know that this isn't my first choice, but nevertheless, not my will but Thine."

THE GOD DOT

The Lord is faithful in everything and I knew this wouldn't be an exception. Whatever happened, I was prepared to lean on the One who is always there, who provides, comforts, empowers, and loves more deeply than anyone else.

Three days later, while I was still camped out at my husband's bedside, the husband of one of my best friends called to tell me that she passed away an hour earlier. After twelve days and an ordeal I wouldn't wish on anyone, my husband finally escaped the hospital. He didn't look the same, didn't act the same, and I didn't expect him to ever be the same as he was two weeks earlier. He was so sick that the nurses had *that look* about them when they returned to work after a few days off. They even said, "He's still here?"

God provides. Months later my husband was back doing his daily chores and we were grateful. During his convalescence I realized that one day I wouldn't be able to do all the work myself.

God Dots mark His active presence in your life. One Dot doesn't tell you much except that you're not alone. My constant companions during these days and weeks were the Father, Son, and Holy Spirit. I was never alone, never in despair, and never doubted His faithfulness. Yet He didn't see fit to offer one clue about what I was to prepare for. Many times over the next few years, I asked if the five-year window was still in play. The answer was always a definite yes, but I never got an answer to the question, "Get ready for what?"

Finally, I figured out that He expected me to move forward and follow the Dots. They would lead me where I needed to go and prepare me for—whatever.

March 14, 2018

This was the day I met JD Smith at Bible study. You'll remember that he and I met for coffee two days later, discovering that we'd each read the other's book(s) the night before and knew that something was afoot. Within two months, he and his wife, Donna, asked my husband and me to enter discipleship with them. Even as I admitted to myself and the Lord that I didn't want to, I knew I had to. This was a God Dot I'd been expecting since the day I met JD. As he told us later, he knew immediately when he walked into the Bible study. Neither of us suspected what came next.

When we met, JD and Donna had two grown children, grown granddaughters, and he enjoyed perfect health with people newly in place to continue his mission. Within four months of the day we met at Bible study, JD was diagnosed with terminal cancer, their only son passed away unexpectedly, and the people lined up to carry on experienced their own life altering situations.

God Dot. God Dot. God Dot.

Sometimes they come so quickly in succession that all you can do is go along and wait for the next one. Eventually, JD and Donna gave me legal copyright for their book and the rights to all their published and unpublished material. As led by the Spirit, I would carry the message forward. A year and a half into our work together I told JD that I was two years into a five-year window to *get ready*. There was still no answer from above, but we both felt that there would be time for us to finish our work together before he passed away.

After months of work, the second edition of their book was published. JD was too frail at the end of the process to review the final manuscript, but the four of us worked together on the new title and cover, and I wrote the foreword. At the end of November 2019, when they could no longer manage in an apartment with just daytime help, JD and Donna moved 125 miles further west to be near their daughter.

On January 20, 2020, I put a copy of the new book in JD's hands. Four days later he moved into hospice care at a nursing home. I visited him a few days later and we closed out the earthly side of our work together as he prepared to move on. That precious time was another God Dot on my journey. JD passed away eleven days later.

Our time with JD and Donna was part of the five-year preparation. I finally realized that I didn't have to figure it out, but that I would be ready for whatever was coming. I stopped asking, trusting that obedience would get me ready. This was in God's hands.

September 3, 2019

We went to bed at the end of a normal day. I don't know if I'd been asleep or not when I knew something was wrong. The first clue came when I heard my husband breathing in moist heaving waves that reminded me of Dad's death rattle. It sounded more like wretches or gurgles than snoring. Hoping that the sound was nothing more than a particularly creative snore, I reached over with my left hand to pat his arm thinking that it might rouse him enough to normalize his breathing.

Nothing changed. The death rattles continued. I'd spent hours with my father, did internet searches at the time to satisfy myself that he wasn't in distress, gave him the medication ordered by the hospice nurse, and sat with him until the rattles ceased.

The sound stopped. The room went quiet. I looked at my husband's head on the pillow, the ambient light from electronic devices bright enough to see his face. I nudged him. Nothing. I shoved him. His eyes were open, staring sightlessly at the ceiling. I got up and walked around to his side of the bed to check for respiration. Before I got there I thought, maybe this is the onset of sleep apnea. But there was no breath, and his face and body were so changed I hardly recognized him.

Then I realized—

"He's dead."

I couldn't believe it. I remember saying aloud, "Is this how it ends?"

I shook him. Then I tried to elicit a pain response. If he was there, he should react.

There was nothing.

At all.

His was not the first dead body I tried to revive. In 1978 a young mother knocked on the door of my condo because she smelled gas in a neighborhood with no gas lines. I went to her house and heard a car in the neighbor's garage that shared a wall with her home. We called to other neighbors, broke the locked door open, and dragged our 40-something-year-old neighbor out of the driver's seat. I pulled on one arm and someone else had the other. The moment she was outside, I knelt and began mouth-to-mouth. Which I would have skipped if I'd taken time to notice that her arms were still up in the air because rigor had already set in.

I took the heel of my left hand and slammed it into my husband's sternum. I figured, if he's dead he won't care and if there's a chance of getting him back, I'll do whatever I can to shock something in his chest back to life. After a minute or so, I may already have called 911, he took a great odd breath from somewhere deep within. One. Then nothing. I waited. The heel of my left hand whacked him on the chest again a few more times. Nothing. There was nothing to wake up.

I waited in the "do not hang up the phone" mode for the ambulance to arrive. Did I hit him in the chest again? I don't know, but there was no one present except me, the dogs, the 911 operator, and the Lord. I was totally calm.

No one knows how long it was, but my husband woke up. All the way. I understood where we were before, but this was outside my area of comprehension. I told the 911 operator. Trying to decide if I should cancel the ambulance or let it come, I made my husband stand up to compare the strength in his right and left hands, then walk to the bedroom door and back to assess his neurological condition. His reactions were equal, and he even walked with more conviction than usual.

He was back and I knew why.

God Dot.

Big God Dot.

I cancelled the ambulance and told my husband that we were going to the Emergency Room to get him checked out. He didn't think it was necessary at first, but once he realized that his body had reacted the way most do when a person passes, he took a shower, I threw the sheets into the washer, and we left. One of the first things I asked him on the way to the stand-alone ER was, "What do you remember?" I was a tad bit disappointed when he answered, "Nothing."

The ER doc agreed that he was gone but that I'd somehow resuscitated him. My answer to that was, "I don't have the power to do that, but I know who does." They decided the event "was a perfect storm of eyedrops and something else." He'd used the same eyedrops for two years. He was admitted to the hospital, and after a myriad of specialists examined and tested him, the *something else* remains a mystery and he's perfectly fine. We know what the something else is. Or rather, who it is.

Even though I thought I did, I didn't understand the extent of coming changes when I knew my time with Journey would end. I accepted that, but nothing short of a miracle could get me out of the barn I'd dreamed about my entire life, the one I believed would be our home and ministry base for the rest of our lives. God Dots come in many varieties and for many reasons. This time we got the message. We got the miracle. The getting ready process for whatever waits at the end of the five-year period includes a huge change in lifestyle. Making it required a huge

God Dot. Two months later we moved into town for the first time in more than thirty years, boarded the remaining two horses, sold the barn, and then COVID-19 hit the world.

One year and one day after my husband's perfect storm, the concept of the God Dot arrived.

No one's world looks the same as it did before the virus. There are God Dots everywhere, but how many recognize them? This book is part of my getting ready process. At the time I'm writing this, the five-year window ends in less than six months. I know part of what will happen, but also know enough to leave plenty of room for God to act again.

Each God Dot in this line sequence was a big one, but taken together it's easy to see the line they form and the direction it points. When you document your Dot Line and fill in as many blank spaces as possible, do you begin to see a pattern? A direction?

I've written my Dots down for years and reviewed notes made at the time each event occurred to organize this chapter. If you haven't done the same, let me encourage you to begin today. Look for God's hand in your life. In the small things as well as the great ones. In the appearance of a white feather, if that's how you know that He's there, or the passing of a loved one. God is always there, always involved, and His Spirit resides within you to guide, comfort, rejoice, exalt, and praise, regardless of the circumstances.

Sometimes God must do big things to change the course you're on because it's a big change. In my rearview mirror I see an endless row of God Dots lined up like little tin soldiers, perfectly organized in rank with not a one out of place.

God Dots... comforting signs from our Heavenly Father. — Salye Coles

SEVENTEEN

"WELL DONE."

His lord said to him, "Well done, good and faithful servant; you were faithful over a few things, I will make you ruler over many things. Enter into the joy of your lord."
Matthew 25:21

On October 14, 2019, my amazing gray gelding, Bo, loaded into the Wings of Hope trailer to begin a new life serving disabled and special children and adults, something he was uniquely qualified to do. Eyes brimming with unshed tears, I watched the truck stop and wait for our automatic gate to open. It turned onto the street and Bo was gone.

Bo came into my life as a two-year-old who'd never worn a halter or received a lesson. His owners considered him a reject because he was born with narcolepsy and a lop ear—and he was gray. At two, he was more of a pasture pet than anything else, following his people anywhere if they had his brand of cookie in their hand. I drooled when I saw his "For Sale" photo online —rose gray with huge dark dapples, black mane and tail, and a huge blaze still visible on his handsome gray face. The photo caught Bo in mid-gallop, his powerful build, athleticism, and substance visible to even the uneducated eye. Two weeks later, Bo followed a cookie into my horse trailer and came home.

Looking back, I recognize the God Dot that drew my attention to Bo's photo. From my first glimpse, I never doubted that I would own and train him, but never dreamed that he would eventually own a part of my heart that is his forever. For eleven years no one saddled or rode Bo but me. He became my work horse, competition horse, ministry horse, clinician partner, and did everything I asked, whenever and wherever I asked. I trusted him without reservation or concern.

No matter what, I never lied to Bo and he never refused to serve. Eventually, I let my husband and two special friends ride him. For all the years he was with me, someone else sat on his back less than a dozen times. I learned from Bo every bit as much as he learned from me and his unique gift was reflecting my relationship with God in a way I could understand. My first book, *Amazing Grays, Amazing Grace*, is about two gray quarter horses—Bo and Swizzle—and the journey we took together as I learned how close the relationship between a human and horse parallels that of a human and God.

One God Dot I'll never forget is the day Bo showed me the puzzling (or irritating) face I sometimes show the Lord. After finishing our lesson, I rode him into the barn, stopping to dismount in front of his stall. I pulled his bridle and walked over to the tack room to hang it up. As expected, Bo remained right where I left him. When I came out of the tack room, I realized that he was thirty feet away. I figured it was easier for him to bring the saddle to me than it was for me to walk over, take it off, and haul it back.

Our eyes met, and I gestured for Bo to walk over to me. "Come" is one of the four basic commands Jesus used with His disciples and one of the same four I teach my horses. Bo didn't need me to say anything because he knew exactly what I asked. When his feet didn't move, I was stunned, because Bo is reliably obedient.

Did he understand what I asked?

Yes, he did.

Was there anything preventing him from coming to me?

No, there wasn't.

Bo looked directly at me, ears forward and interested, his eyes soft and content. Nothing about his body language suggested resistance, discomfort, confusion, or discontent. Yet, his feet didn't move in my direction.

"What's wrong with you? You know precisely what I want, it's easy to do, and you're happy and content in our relationship—so why don't you come?"

Another God Dot dropped into place when I realized how many times I must have shown this same face to God. If He didn't already know the answer, which He does, He might have asked me, *What's wrong with you? You know precisely what I want, it's easy to do, and you're happy and content in our relationship—so why don't you come?*

I don't know how many times Bo served as a God Dot messenger, but they were many and there were more to come. In my plan, Bo and I would live under the same roof together until separated by death. As it turned out, my plan and God's weren't the same. After my husband died and was returned to me, we knew that life was about to change. Whatever new mission God had for us would take us out of my beloved barn. For the first time in more than thirty years, I would not live with horses. Somehow, I knew that God would leave me two horses, and I was content to let Him choose which two, believing that Bo would be one of them.

God wastes nothing and knows the path ahead better than we ever will. In late September, during my private time with the Lord, the message came that Bo should go to Wings of Hope, a wonderful ministry offering equine-assisted therapy to clients with physical and developmental challenges. We already had one horse there and knew that Bo could serve on a bigger stage for years to come and be cherished as he deserved. My husband agreed that it was the right decision. Over the years, I learned that the best place to be is in God's will, and if that meant that Bo should go to Wings of Hope, then that is how it would be. This was a momentous decision for me personally that I thought would functionally end my equine ministry and could never be undone, so I asked the Lord for confirmation.

It arrived. In spades. Big God Dot. I was to let Bo go, and I agreed. But it's not always that simple. During quiet time a week later, I reminded God, as if He needed it, that letting Bo go was huge and could I please have confirmation again? After all, Gideon asked twice, once for a wet fleece and once for a dry (Judges 6:36-40). Again, I received an immediate response.

The next God Dot was a bit different. Another week passed and I still didn't call Wings of Hope to even ask if they wanted Bo. I went back to the well for a third time, asking for confirmation just one more time. The answer was just as direct but delivered in an entirely different voice. The message was clear, *You're getting dangerously close to disobedience.*

Two minutes later I made the call and set a date for the director to come get Bo.

Many agree that everything they have is a gift on loan from God. Except for salvation, everything else comes with a time frame. Bo was a gift God asked me to return, to serve where God wanted him to. Surprisingly, there was no sense of loss or discontent in the moment because I trust Jesus with my today and my eternity, and I trust Him with Bo. The words, "Well done, good and faithful servant," rang in my ears. God let me know how pleased He was with the way I'd multiplied the value of this beautiful creature who made my life far richer than it could have been without him. Without my husband and Bo, I wouldn't be who I am today. Several horses left hoof prints on my heart and changed the course of my life, but Bo has no competition for who carried me the furthest. He took me to places I never dreamed I could go. I still refuse to dwell on his absence because I love him today as much as ever.

The instant the trailer carrying Bo away turned out of our driveway, God delivered a Dot of revelation I'll cherish forever. Leaving the barn that I loved more than any place I've lived in my life wouldn't be as hard as I thought. When Bo passed beyond the border of our property, I realized that I'd designed and built the entire place for him. But for that God Dot, I wouldn't have believed it. Bo would be fine, he would continue to serve, God would watch over him, and God was pleased with me.

Jesus Christ promises soul rest to all who walk the path He chooses—the one made visible by His markers. Once Bo was gone, packing everything up from my life with horses wasn't as difficult as it could have been. We lived under the same roof as our horses, the horse side a short fourteen second walk from our bedroom or my office. The first thing I saw when I opened the door was Bo, who always knew when I was coming out. He's the only horse who never changed stalls in all the years we lived there. We sold the barn to a family God sent who will cherish and steward it well. The only thing I said goodbye to the day we turned the property over to the new owners was Bo's empty stall.

I turned away and didn't look back.

God Dots: *When He pops in unexpectedly.* — Stacy Thacker

EIGHTEEN
THE PATH FORWARD

God gives dreams and visions through you, not to you. They aren't possessions but something you experience and bring to life. Develop the habit of looking for God because He's always with you. In those moments when you feel like you're out of His presence, it's not because He isn't there, but because either you're not tuned in or you suffer from distraction.

Create your God Dot map going backward, recognizing, savoring, and connecting each message and moment that God made Himself known to you. Practice ordering and visualizing the picture your Dots create. Own the reality of God's order and know that He acts in your life every day. God Dots teach you to see Him and recognize the ways He shows up.

You were created to dream dreams, see visions, and bring God's kingdom to the earth. Heavenly power comes through you by the Holy Spirit. It's not your power, but you carry it into the world to do His will, accomplish His purpose, and act or speak in ways that achieve His plan for you. Transformation has no delete key.

Whether you're eight or eighty-eight, you are here with purpose. God has a path and vision for you. The goal is simple and singular, that you become undivided in focus, making relationship to Him the first thing in your life, not something shoehorned into your free time. Until then, He can't accomplish the unique part of His plan that works through you.

With each passing day, your line of Dots left to discover is shorter, and God doesn't have as much time to get you where He needs you to be, securely on that narrow road, that path of Dots that is yours alone and leads to the narrow gate to eternity with Christ. It's easy to say, "Oh, it's too late, I'm too old" and give yourself a pass. I understand how tempting it is because I've thought about using the same excuse. My body has issues, gravity is real, and sometimes it's both the age and the miles.

Shouldn't I just accept reality? My husband is older than I am, there's a pandemic, I get by, but am not exactly a technical whiz kid. At my age, how am I supposed to do what God showed me still lies ahead?

Doesn't He know?

You already know what a ridiculous question that is.

Recognizing God Dots is your responsibility, not the Dot Creator's. If He can't trust you to notice the small markers He leaves, why expect to see big ones? The scope of your vision and purpose expands every time you see more of what already is. God won't get bigger or more obvious if you aren't watching and listening now. Even when you're fully at the watch you'll miss some major Dots. But if you keep looking, He'll be faithful to help you see more.

God's teaching isn't for yesterday or tomorrow, but for now. Your connection and value to Him isn't for someday, but today. Put the pursuit of relationship off for a more convenient time and your choice of what's most important to you becomes clear —it isn't God. Jesus repeated and expanded the clear message of the new covenant first announced in Jeremiah 31:31. You can't fool God because He judges what's in your heart, not just behavior that can be seen.

Everything He gives is for your blessing and His benefit, to bring you closer and make you one with Jesus as Jesus is one with His Father. Do you believe God gives or does anything with the intent to separate you from Him? That sounds like a message from the opposition, not the Holy Spirit.

"Obedient unto death," not "obedient in the convenient."

FOR MONTHS I studied the pecan trees along the walking trail each morning while chatting with God. Then odd things began to happen. Every tree was laden with half-ripe pecans, all very normal and average, and I looked forward to scavenging a few pecans when they ripened. Then one by one the trees dropped their fruit. Not gradually, but overnight, and all without a trace of the pecans to be found. Except for one tree. While the others were now barren, with leaves turning to brown and curling on the edges, one tree was still heavy with fruit, vibrant green, and healthy as it could be. Recording every change, new notes and photographs joined my growing Pecan Chronicle.

A week earlier I'd read Tomi Arayoni's book, *Eat, Sleep, Prophesy, Repeat,* which encourages believers to grow in their ability to hear the voice of God in a prophetic way. It seemed both timely and natural to wonder if the pecan situation had something to do with the church or the timeline of human history, because that's how I think. A few weeks later, the one healthy tree was also fruitless except for one beautiful green pecan on a low-hanging branch within my reach. The tree next to it, probably planted the same day, was losing its leaves and appeared worn out. This became my Prophecy Pecan because I expected to learn something of note through my daily visits and observations. Not only did I anticipate a lesson, but I believed God would give me that last pecan when it was ripe. I wanted and expected to add the Prophecy Pecan itself to weeks of notes and countless photographs.

My Prophecy Pecan was on the tree December fourth but gone on the fifth. The point where it attached to the tree was fresh wood, but the pecan was either gone or hiding in the tall grass and blanket of fallen leaves around the base. Believe me, I looked for it and I have the pictures. The next day I searched again but knew I wouldn't find the pecan and why. Even though I was disappointed, there is a lesson, and it came at precisely the time I needed it.

God Dots are unexpected, not something you document, anticipate, and expect for months in advance. My God Dot for the day provided greater clarity. The special moments when

God makes Himself known in your life are unexpected, personal, intimate, and powerful. He doesn't take requests.

I confess, I don't have all the answers about God Dots, but I know they aren't a specific answer to prayer or part of an ongoing conversation you have with the Lord. They're unexpected, which begs the question, how do you expect the unexpected? The more you anticipate God's markers in your life the more you see. God makes Himself known in many ways. The closest illustration I can think of is the return of Jesus Christ. You know He's coming back; you know where and how He's returning, but you can't know the day or hour. Like the wise virgins of Matthew 25:1-13, you must be ready with trimmed lamps and a full supply of oil so when the moment arrives, you'll be welcomed in to the wedding.

Train your brain to seek out God Dots. Expect the unexpected but don't do what I did with the Prophecy Pecan and choose the marker you think will look best on your Dot Line. God Dots arrive perfectly timed and personally chosen by the One who knows you better than you know yourself, proving that you're always loved and never alone.

> *And when these things begin to come to pass, then look up, and lift up your heads; for your redemption draws near.* — Luke 21:28

Just because God brings you somewhere you expect Him to, it doesn't mean that it's your last stop. Most of your stops are intermediate destinations. Many places that feel like home are only resting places. The Lord wants to reward you, encourage you, and compliment you with, "Well done." But since you're still breathing, there's more road ahead. God brought Journey into my life and took him out again because I learned the lessons he brought, and it was time for both of us to serve in new ways.

The past few decades were packed with growth. Just when I thought I was where God wanted me to be, accepting and becoming comfortable with one new role, He changed things up. *Well done*, but now it's time to move up a step, over a step, or back a step. I think I finally get it.

If you're where the Lord wants you today, it's a win. Yesterday is in the vault and tomorrow never really arrives—it just becomes a new today. God's plan for you includes many pivots, stages, and lessons. When you look back at the end of your life, I expect you'll see fat, neon-lit God Dots at each intersection.

Watch for imposter dots, those apparent coincidences the ruler of this world wants you to believe come from God. Remember that genuine God Dots agree with His Word, are unexpected, have purpose, connect to each other—and they always point you directly to the God of the Bible. Genuine God Dots offer hope, vision, and a path forward. They offer an opportunity to see where you've come from and where you're going by the way they mark His presence and participation in everyday events. Christians who worry, harbor faith-eroding fear, or live with insecurity about the state of the world today have the power to uncover new stores of soul rest, confidence, and freedom by discovering God's vision and purpose for them. One God Dot is a beginning.

Light will defeat darkness, revealing how the world plays us and why we've fallen for it. Two amazing words coupled together clear the path for something bigger, more powerful, and more blessed: *until now*. Whatever your history, that's only your story until now. This moment is a new now, a fresh chapter and opportunity to wipe the slate clean and begin to seek God wherever He may be found. Expect to see Him everywhere and in everything.

All that Jesus promised is available to you today, from the protection of His armor to facing the "ruler of this world" with confidence, knowledge, and victory. Don't be concerned about your weakness or limitations because the power, purpose, and potential are His. You may stand tall and firm because you know to whom you belong and you're ready to "see" the path forward. Joy and peace aren't for someday, but for today.

Every morning I walk the same trail with the woods and a creek on one side and suburbia on the other. Time on the trail is precious, reminding me of the lyrics to my father's favorite hymn:

I come to the garden alone
While the dew is still on the roses
And the voice I hear falling on my ear
The Son of God discloses.
And He walks with me
And He talks with me
And He tells me I am His own.
And the joy we share as we tarry there
None other has ever known.
—*Charles Austin Miles*

The deadline to send the manuscript for this book to the editor was less than a week away and I didn't have what I needed to finish. That morning I asked the Father, Son, and Spirit for guidance, inspiration, and a brisk wind at my back to carry the project across the finish line. A few Dots were still missing, and I didn't know where to look for them because Dots are unexpected—quite the conundrum when you face a deadline.

What warms my heart most about intimacy with the Lord is how He makes Himself known in the oddest ways—a feather or melody to some, a rainbow or butterfly to others. The God Dot that greeted me on the walking trail after that prayer was a huge sewer access, its thirty-inch diameter, forged manhole cover elevated on an even wider, blunt-topped concrete pyramid, and a four-foot tall flat-stock iron marker noting the location, the top of which was painted brilliant yellow on one side and vibrant teal on the other. One would think it would be obvious.

What was different from the two times a day I'd walked past the manhole cover for a year was that day was the first time I saw the monstrous beast crouching all of two feet from the mowed, paved trail. My RAS filter sought out things of God and His creation along the trail. I was ever curious about which woodland companions I'd meet—deer, squirrels, a variety of birds, changes in trees and their color, noticing flowers that weren't there the day before, following pecans and acorns as they appear and disappear, searching the ground, surroundings, and sky for the smallest sign of God's presence and plan. My eyes spent more time looking at the wooded side than the open backyards, but wouldn't you'd think that at least once in a few hundred trips I'd have noticed the honking industrial intruder?

How did I completely miss this monster? This was distraction dementia of the best kind because I saw the things of God and not those of man. God Dots teach you to seek out more Dots and ignore what offers nothing of value to your walk in the garden. Instead of seeing manhole covers, I listened for the voice of God and experienced the joy of His intimate companionship.

Guard against distraction dementia of the worst kind, those distractions that highlight the world and hide God, by expecting the unexpected, which is, I know, oxymoronic. How do you explain two opposites existing simultaneously? God Dots never appear without reason and are always timely, which explains my experience on the walking trail that day.

My prayer on the walking trail the next day was much the same, asking for help to finish this book. How should it end? I didn't know, but I'll provide witness that when you seek or ask you really will find or receive, even though it's feels like a new discovery every time it happens. At least it does to me.

Two days after noticing the manhole covers, I walked under a vividly blue sky which is a rare sight in humid Texas. Radiant sunshine and a small breeze intensified the ambiance of the moment. The golds, warm browns, russets, and reds of mid-December leaves popped against the cloudless azure backdrop. I started feeling too warm, the blue fleece scarf wound around my neck, doubled gloves, and winter coat absorbing the sun and creating too much heat for comfort. Before I had time to unbundle, I felt a slight breeze on my face, the only body part that wasn't covered, and I was immediately chilled and shivering.

God Dot.

When concentrating on the sun I was too hot, but when I thought of the breeze, I was too cold. How is it possible to shift from hot to cold to hot by simply changing what I think about? As my thoughts flipped from sun to breeze to sun, so did my thermometer. This, I thought, is what it's like to experience both sides of a coin at the same time. You only see the one you focus on, but the other is as present and real as its opposite.

How can two extremes exist simultaneously? Maybe they don't really, but I asked for help and the Holy Spirit provided.

This is what it means to expect the unexpected. You see whatever is uppermost in your mind. I acknowledged the sun and was hot. I felt the wind and was cold. In the shade of the trees there was only cold because their remaining canopy hid the sun. In its absence, the weather was too cold for comfort, yet just a few yards ahead where the sun blanketed the trail, it was balmy, beautiful, warm, and I was overdressed.

God Dots train us to seek that which is above, to look for God and expect to find Him always and everywhere. To see His hand in the mundane as well as the miraculous. God Dots offers hope, vision, and a path forward as you learn how to look backward to see where God marked His presence and participation in your everyday life. Christians who worry, harbor fear that erodes faith, and live with insecurity about the state of the world today will find soul rest, confidence, and freedom by discovering God's unique vision and purpose for them.

Light will defeat darkness and you will see when you were played and how you fell for it—until now. Begin writing your new story today. You'll know God on a deeper level, believe that Jesus's promises are available to you today, and learn how to suit up in the full armor of God. You'll be prepared to face the ruler of this world victoriously with knowledge, peace, and power because you know where you've been. You'll look forward to the path ahead and commit to remember whose you are.

God Dots bring clarity and confidence.

God Dots bring power and peace.

God Dots are unexpected but expect them anyway.

Your last God Dot is the moment you enter eternity with Jesus Christ.

...

NOTES

2. The God Dot

1. https://www.techrepublic.com/article/apple-iphone-11-a-cheat-sheet/
2. vanseodesign.com, July 12, 2010

11. Dot Blindness

1. https://www.livescience.com/6727-invisible-gorilla-test-shows-notice.html#:~:text=Of%20the%2041%20volunteers%20Simon,ape%20in%20the%20new%20experiment.
2. https://www.youtube.com/watch?v=vJG698U2Mvo
3. https://www.youtube.com/watch?v=IGQmdoK_ZfY

12. Distraction Dementia

1. https://medium.com/desk-of-van-schneider/if-you-want-it-you-might-get-it-the-reticular-activating-system-explained-761b6ac14e53
2. https://www.nytimes.com/2011/08/21/magazine/do-you-suffer-from-decision-fatigue.html

ABOUT THE AUTHOR

Lynn Baber is a Christian author, teacher, and speaker helping others discover and release the power, authority, and confidence God places in them for His purpose. She combines God's truth with daily life, using creative illustrations and sometimes a bit of humor.

A World and National Champion horse trainer and breeder, Lynn judged shows in the US and Europe. Among her book titles is the Gospel Horse Series, four best-selling books promoting relationship with God, horses, and one another that few experience.

Lynn works to connect believers with God's constant presence in their daily lives through books, Bible studies, and sharing practical gospel-based skills. She's also worked with ministries, equine therapy barns, leaders, authors, and as a teaching cheerleader for business owners and non-profits.

She invites you to join the private THE GOD DOT Facebook group and share the journey. Connect with Lynn at www.LynnBaber.com.

OTHER BOOKS BY LYNN BABER

The Gospel Horse Series

Amazing Grays, Amazing Grace

He Came Looking for Me

Discipleship with Horses

The Breath of Horse Crazy

Other Titles

Rapture and Revelation

Fifteen Minutes into Eternity

The Art of Getting to YES

Expect the unexpected.
THE GOD DOT.
See and hear Him today.

www.ingramcontent.com/pod-product-compliance
Lightning Source LLC
Chambersburg PA
CBHW050317120526
44592CB00014B/1950